Restoring Order

Vicki Norris

HARVEST HOUSE PUBLISHERS

EUGENE, OREGON

D0150212

Cover by Terry Dugan Design, Minneapolis, Minnesota
Front and back cover author photos © ajsstudio.com

RESTORING ORDER
Copyright © 2006 by Vicki Norris
Published by Harvest House Publishers
Eugene, Oregon 97402
www.harvesthousepublishers.com

Library of Congress Cataloging-in-Publication Data
Norris, Vicki, 1973-
    Restoring order / Vicki Norris.
        p. cm.
    Includes bibliographical references.
    ISBN-13: 978-0-7369-1647-9 (pbk.)
    ISBN-10: 0-7369-1647-4
    1. Stewardship, Christian. 2. Christian life. I. Title.
    BV772.N67 2006
    248'.6—dc22   2005022898

Printed in the United States of America

06 07 08 09 10 11 12 13 14 /DP-KB/ 10 9 8 7 6 5 4 3 2

I dedicate this book with thanks...

To God, for giving me an unwavering belief that all things are possible for me.

To my husband, Trevor, for helping me to savor the present while I strive for the future.

To my granny, Grace, for letting me organize her purse and dresser and anything else I could get my hands on when I was little.

To my parents, for supporting me and believing in me.

To my Restoring Order® team, for partnering with me to transform lives.

To our clients, who have taught me that order really can liberate our lives.

Contents

A Note from the Author.................... 7

Part One: Organizing Truths

1. Life Management 13
2. The Disorder Debt 31
3. The Disorder Disease 47
4. No Shortcuts to Order 61
5. The Freedom Factor 79

Part Two: Organizing Principles

6. The Priority Principle 97
7. The Process Principle 111
8. The Pain Principle....................... 125
9. The Preparation Principle................. 141
10. The Pruning Principle.................... 153
11. The Possibility Principle.................. 165

Part Three: Organizing Strategies

12. Dig Out and Dig In 179
13. Take an Aerial View 195
14. Purpose Your Space 209
15. Getting Started 223
16. The Secret to Maintenance................ 235
    Notes 253

A Note from the Author

Dear Friends,

I wrote this book for those who are ready for change. If you are tired of being overwhelmed and thwarted by your disorganization, you are not alone. Perhaps you've tried all the latest quick tips and products to control clutter but to no avail. Before you give up, I want to encourage you to hold on to your hope! As a seasoned professional organizer who has been in the trenches, I've seen literally hundreds of people restore order to their lives. If you are prepared to discover how you became disorganized in the first place and to practice new behaviors, you are a candidate for transformation.

Too often, we seek immediate gratification and expect instant impact for our organizing efforts. That's why we turn to the overly simplistic tricks and "three simple steps" that we find in most magazines and on many bookstore shelves. We want to find a Band-Aid for our disorganization. We dive in, madly sorting and tossing, feeling as if we're doing something to fend off the tidal wave headed our way. We take shortcuts rather than expending educated effort to find real solutions. Those of us who have tried these shortcutting methods know that the "fire, aim, ready" approach never works.

When we start organizing, we tend to put tactics before reason. We see a messy space and launch a wild, full frontal assault before we understand the background of the problem and equip ourselves to meet the challenge. This is like going into battle unarmed without knowing our enemy!

Understanding should always precede action, so I have organized this book in a way that puts first things first. One of my favorite proverbs demonstrates that applied knowledge should come after wisdom: "By wisdom a house is built, and through understanding it is established; through knowledge its rooms are filled with rare and beautiful treasures" (Proverbs 24:3-4). Using this model for our structure, we'll begin with part 1: Organizing Truths, proceed to part 2: Organizing Principles, and wrap up with part 3: Organizing Strategies.

In part 1: Organizing Truths, you'll see that practicing order is good life management. I compare being disorganized to being in debt or having a disease. I talk about the shortcuts that people take to getting organized and why they don't work. I finish part 1 by drawing the connection between order and freedom.

In part 2: Organizing Principles, I share six key concepts for change. All the principles for transformation start with the letter *P*: priority, process, pain, preparation, pruning, and possibility. Some of the principles are catalysts for organizing, and the rest show how to get from here to there.

The organizing truths and principles prepare you for part 3: Organizing Strategies. If you've been salivating for an organizing makeover, you'll pick up proven methods for digging out and digging in. You'll learn how to take an "aerial view" of your environment and "purpose" your space for better utilization. You will discover assessment strategies and get started with your project. Finally, you'll uncover the secret to maintaining the order you've created.

In this book, I purposely resist offering you quick tips and how-to advice. You're probably more interested in getting freedom from your disorganization than collecting another useless trick. I've observed that no one-size-fits-all solution exists, so I'm sharing with you a discovery process that you can use to resolve your own unique organizing challenges. I will help you figure out how you got here so you can dig down and pull out the root of your disorganization weed.

If you take the time to absorb these organizing truths and principles before you race to make changes in your environment, your efforts will be far more likely to last. If you read this book from start to finish, you will be equipped to make room in your life for your priorities. This book is a resource that you can return to whenever you need to restore order. Get out your highlighter, write in the margins, and turn down the pages. Make this book your own and claim those nuggets that apply to you. You will acquire a proven process for organizing, a new definition of success, and a liberated, reclaimed life!

Part One

Organizing Truths

1

Life Management

Her face went pale when she got the call. She argued and pleaded, but the coach was firm. It wasn't his fault, he explained. All the other parents got their forms in on time. Her son just wouldn't be able to play on the football team this year because all the places had been filled. But he'd been on the team for years, she reminded the coach. He was a good kid. It wasn't even his fault! But the coach could do nothing...the team was full.

The Disordered Life

Mary was deflated when she hung up the phone. She is a busy executive who logs 60 to 80 hour workweeks, travels for business, and is raising three children. Like most moms, Mary is running at mach speed and is drowning in paper and responsibilities at home. She had simply set aside the football team sign-up form. Now she couldn't even find it. Mary frequently misplaces important papers and spends countless hours searching for documents. She feels stress and terrible guilt about the backlog of paper and clutter at home. She just doesn't have time to deal with the paper piles. Now, however, someone else had to pay for her chaotic mess. How was she going to tell her son? How was she going to tell her husband that they'd have to sit this season out?

We've all heard that being disorganized costs us time and money, which indeed it does, but as Mary's misfortune demonstrates, living in chaos can bring much greater costs to our lifestyle and state of mind. When we live on the edge all the time, we lose out on many important things in our life.

Pay As You Go

When Mary hired me to help dig her out of chaos at home and at work, she told me that she felt the clutter in her life was trapping her in the "pay as you go" system. To her, the "pay as you go" system meant experiencing the consequences of her disorder on a daily basis.

Mary was not only disorganized at home; her office at work was also replete with organization problems. Her hand-me-down desk ate up the entire office and was covered in stacks of paper. A self-confessed piler, Mary simply heaped projects onto the floor in stacks when she ran out of surface space. Insufficient lighting and a depressing environment didn't help. Mary had purchased every office supply she could think of to manage her projects and deadlines but to no avail. Her bulletin board was covered in layers of reminders that used to mean something. She knew that her disorganization caused redundancy in individual project files as well as her jam-packed filing cabinet.

Mary constantly faced the negative impact of her chaos as she looked for lost documents, missed deadlines, and continually came up short. She told me that more than anything she wanted to feel "on top of things." She wanted to be able to respond quickly to questions that people asked her, rather than searching for the answers and feeling inadequate. She was living her professional life reactively, unable to fulfill her potential. Mary was paying the price for her disorganization every single day.

Nickeled-and-Dimed

Another time we talked, Mary compared her disorder to being cheated. She said she felt nickeled-and-dimed by her particular brand of chaos. The paper piles at work and at home were grating on her nerves and causing all kinds of problems, including the trouble with the football team sign-up sheet. Mary was experiencing tremendous pain from her inadequate paper management.

Mary's checkbook accounting was always falling behind because she hated bothering with it. Instead of unraveling the confusion in her account, she would close her checking account and open another one, leaving a small balance just in case something unexpected cleared the account. She did this without her husband's knowledge because he left their finances, like most things, up to Mary to handle on her own. Her opening-and-closing habits precipitated an ever-growing list of account numbers and a flood of mail with multiple checking account statements. Poor Mary—her paper piles caused financial mismanagement, and her financial misman-agement caused even more paper piles!

The financial confusion wasn't limited to her checking account. Mary also didn't have a good bill-paying system and often lost her bills, incurring late fees. Her husband must not know about the late fees, she told me; he would hit the roof if he knew. She hated writing checks to pay for her tardiness.

She spent hundreds of dollars, maybe even thousands, every year on late fees. She hated to think of the clothes she could have bought or vacations her family could have taken with that money. Ashamed of herself, she didn't want her husband to find out how much money she was continuing to waste. She knew she could prevent this needless expense if she just took the time to figure out a better system.

Mary was at the height of frustration when she called me. She was beginning to let her family down as a result of her disorganization. She was disappointing herself and her boss with her ineffective project management. Mary was hiding her habits and wasting valuable family resources. Instead of being in control of her life, her disoriented environment and lack of systems controlled her. She had created her own chaos and was totally overwhelmed.

Like Mary, many of us feel plagued and cheated by an unruly environment. We have nonexistent or unmanageable systems. A wave of paper is taking over our homes and our offices with ever-increasing volume. Our financial management is poor as we try in vain to keep up with all the statements, accounts, bills, and receipts. Our financial struggles and paper pileup are separate but related problems that compound one another. We hate feeling so out-of-control, yet our frantic pace tricks us into believing we can't slow down long enough to fix our own problems. Even if we don't understand the implications of our chaotic lifestyle, we long for a better way to live.

The Ordered Life

Kathy is a local entrepreneur who always has several irons in the fire. She loves her work and diligently presses hard during office hours. In addition to her career, she participates financially in a couple of start-up companies around town. You could call her a serial entrepreneur because even though she is chief executive officer of a Web design service company, she can't help investing in other good ideas. Her friends come to her with their wild ideas, and she very often turns those ideas into profitability. Whether she is running her design firm or reviewing a business plan, she seems to have boundless energy.

But Kathy is not just interested in work. She is a committed philanthropist who gives back financially to her church and to charities. She loves to read, and she collects the works of her favorite authors. She loves seeing her friends, going to movies, and enjoying the arts. She always seems to have time to go to a show, volunteer at church, or attend a gallery opening. Her kids are grown, but she sees them and their families often. Kathy and her husband travel frequently; they consider vacations the payoff for hard work. Their favorite thing to do is visit all the new restaurants in town for dinner dates. Having a full life and enjoying her time with family and friends is important to Kathy. She values having balance in her professional, personal, familial, and spiritual life.

Calendar Care

Many of you are probably thinking that having a life as full and balanced as Kathy's would be nice, and you may be wondering, *How does she do it?* Kathy runs a tight ship. From dawn till dusk, Kathy's day is planned. Her calendar is full from seven in the morning till nine at night, and she manages it carefully. Since her college years, Kathy has always used a planner and to-do lists. She accomplishes a lot because she is organized with her time and tasks.

Kathy isn't just organized with her time; she is purposeful. Her executive assistant helps her sort through the pile of invitations and appointment requests and prioritize them for her acceptance or regrets. Kathy knows that if she says yes to everything, she will no longer be in charge of her own life. She has to decline many opportunities so that she can keep her work and her start-up companies in a primary position of importance.

In addition to exercising restraint with opportunities, Kathy demonstrates self-control with her own workload as well. She dedicates the first and last half hour of each day to planning and organizing. She involves her assistant whenever possible to keep her accountable and on task. She sets this daily "processing time" as an appointment on her calendar. Making herself plow through requests and paper and projects isn't always easy, but she does it because she is committed to staying on top of things. Other important tasks do not bump her daily processing appointments; she considers planning as important as meeting with an investor. Kathy understands the value of work-flow management.

As far as her personal life goes, she schedules events with her husband and children first and then populates her calendar with fun activities with friends. Kathy has learned that if she waits to fit family activities into her schedule, they will always be trumped by other pressing demands. Kathy enjoys her career and her social life because she has proactively made choices to schedule and stick to her priorities.

Financial Care

We can easily think that other folks have it made. We look at their lives and think that things are somehow easier for them than they are for us. Kathy has the money to afford a lifestyle of professional and personal fulfillment, we reason, so life is easier for her. After all, people who make executive salaries can justify a life of travel and entertainment. *It must be nice,* we think to ourselves.

Actually, Kathy and her husband give generously to their church and other causes, and they choose to live fairly modestly. They live in a three-bedroom home so they have room for the grandkids to visit, but they don't live in luxury. They live comfortably within their means. Using their money to reflect their values is important to them.

Kathy spends a half day every week managing the information produced by her start-up companies and tracking their financial situation. She keeps a file on each of her invested companies and stays in touch with the principals. She doesn't just throw money at these ventures; she actually spends time managing her involvement in them.

Similarly, Kathy's husband, Rod, spends several hours a week managing their investments and their paperwork. He reads and files financial statements and keeps their home office in order. He retrieves his and Kathy's receipts and enters them into a financial software program. Together, Rod and Kathy take their financial responsibilities seriously. To them, good financial oversight allows them to do the things they love in their personal life, like going out to dinner and traveling.

People Care

Kathy has held former jobs where she was burdened by an unrealistic workload and ill-equipped staff. She vowed never to experience a work environment like that again. She is in charge of the Web design firm, so she created an environment in which she could thrive. Kathy has sacrificed a healthy part of her own salary in order to make good hires. She recruited an experienced operations manager, a chief financial officer, and an executive assistant. Her assistant helps her keep her office organized so Kathy can work at full capacity. Kathy understands that competent and empowered staff will release her to spend her time wisely.

Delegating is not just a skill that Kathy employs at work. At home, Kathy and Rod make similar choices. Like the rest of us, they do weekly chores like laundry, bookkeeping, and grocery shopping. However, they dedicate a part of their income to hiring a housecleaning service and a lawn service. They are willing to do other maintenance chores, but they don't want to spend their personal time scrubbing toilets or weeding. They don't feel badly about spending money on a housekeeper or gardener because they use their reclaimed time to play with their grandchildren or volunteer at church. Kathy and Rod see both services as an exchange of value. They trade a small portion of their hard-earned income for quality of life.

By making use of other people's skills, Kathy expands her own bandwidth to invest in the things that matter to her. She manages her time and finances well and wants to invest those resources in professional and personal activities that add meaning to her life. Instead of feeling guilty for not being able to do it all, Kathy knows that doing it all is an impossible and foolish undertaking. She would rather work in her strengths than in her weaknesses.

Because she invests in people to support her, Kathy enjoys coming into work and not feeling overwhelmed. She is free to do the things that chief executive officers of small companies are supposed to do, like generate business and manage the company. In former jobs where she was ill-supported, she wore all the hats and could never get on top of things. She also enjoys coming home to a clean home with a well-tended yard. Kathy doesn't need a fancy house or a luxury car; she enjoys the simple pleasures of feeling accomplished at work and being wrapped in comfort at home.

Invest in Order

Are you a Mary or are you a Kathy? Do you have a life of chaos and frustration or a life of self-control and purpose? Most disorganized people are like Mary; their disorder is causing them tremendous pain in their professional and personal life. They long for a life like Kathy's where they could master their time and resources, yet they wonder how they could create a seemingly utopian life like that out of their current situation. Presently, their disorganization is stealing their time, and they always feel behind. They may want help out of the chaos, but at the same time, their anxiety and poor coping methods prevent them from dedicating the time to digging out of their mess.

A disordered life can only become an ordered life when commitment takes charge of chaos. If we want to extricate ourselves from disorganization, we will have to change ourselves. We will have to accept that our mess is not confined to our space and our time management; it extends to our *self*-management. Our disorganization is about our choices. Like Mary, we're in deep waters, and we need a lifeline to get out. We need to reclaim our lives!

Do you know the difference between spending and investing? I never paid much attention to these words until I became a professional organizer and discovered the connection between investing and order. These financial terms can show us our commitment level in almost any area of our life.

Spending is an activity. We spend money when we go to the mall and purchase clothes. We spend our time when we watch television. Spending indicates a trade. We trade our resources for something in return. We can spend thoughtlessly because spending doesn't require much thought.

Investing, on the other hand, is not an activity; it is a purposeful choice. We invest our money in a mutual fund or a retirement account because we are preparing and planning ahead. We are saving for the future. We are choosing to sacrifice our temporary comfort for our long-term gain. Similarly, we invest our time in things that we have deemed important, like being active parents or spouses. Playing with our children and cultivating our marriages are both investment choices. Investing implies that we gain more than we put in; we receive a dividend for our investment. Spending executes a trade, but investing offers a reward.

If you are truly ready to change your ways, then you will need to invest in order. Chances are you've *spent* time and money on organizing in the past but with little reward. You may have spent time tidying up the playroom only to experience a toy explosion the very next day. You may have spent money on a plethora of plastic bins, thinking that products would answer your organizing problems. By spending your time and money on organizing, you've likely accomplished no more than a temporary trade-off. If you realize that your spending has made little or no impact, now is the time to begin investing. When you invest in organizing, you experience a reward for your efforts.

Pay Up Front

In contrast to Mary's "pay as you go" system, in which she felt dinged by her disorder every day, you can operate another way. But as with any other investment, to invest in order, you will have to make an up-front contribution. The good news is that you're investing in yourself. Your up-front contribution will be twofold.

First, you will need to learn about authentic organizing. You wouldn't invest in a stock without researching it and knowing its background. In the same way, you should understand the nature of true organizing before you dive in and make an investment. Our fast-paced world has a skewed view of organizing that values speed and immediate impact. The problem with this approach to organizing is that the results don't last very long.

Authentic organizing is a process, not an activity. It is an organic discovery process that enhances your self-awareness and helps you create systems that work with your lifestyle. Because organizing is a process, not a quick fix, you'll have to dedicate time and resources to the process. You don't make a front-end investment without dedicating time to study it. Likewise, you cannot make an investment without resources like money and energy. Investing requires a commitment of time, finances, and energy.

In the learning process, you'll find that true organizing might be a little painful because it requires that you examine how you became disorganized. Through some introspection and strategy you can resolve the roots of your problems rather than simply addressing the symptoms. Engaging in a genuine organizing process might also be a little painful because you will need to evaluate your habits, behavior, and choices. If you are willing to learn about and embrace organization in the same way you would any other investment, you will be on your way to lasting change.

Second, your up-front investment entails establishing some new systems in your life. By applying a discovery process, you may find some areas that need improvement in your space, time, and task management. You will likely need to implement some systems to help you manage your belongings or your schedule more effectively. Perhaps you have existing systems that you need to tweak, and this is the time to make those adjustments. Your up-front investment in organization must include the creation of viable systems.

Kathy and Rod understand the importance of systems. They did not come about their careful financial management by accident. They took the time to create systems that would help them manage their income and expenses. For example, they sat down together and created a family budget. They added up their monthly income, deducted their church tithes and offerings, allocated funds for savings, and then set an account and a budget for each kind of expense. Their family budget took a little research and time, but that discovery process led to a budget that they felt represented their values. Allocating their money, starting with their priorities of planned giving and savings, allowed them to live their priorities. To go along with their budget, they established a system of capturing, coding, and tracking their receipts. Systems like a family budget and receipt management take a little time to set up, but they are up-front investments in your daily quality of life.

Stay in Sync

After you've made the up-front contribution in your investment process, you will want to do what all investors do: Watch your investments! Like an observant account manager, you will track the changes you've made and keep them operating at peak performance. This is the maintenance stage of organizing. No savvy investor researches a stock, contributes heavily, and then removes all interest. Wise managers are involved at every stage and maintain their investment. When something slides, action is required. Maintaining your investment in organization will require that you continue to observe yourself, your choices, and your systems.

Kathy lives and breathes by her calendar. A lot of people claim they don't want to be tied down like that, but scheduling her priorities first actually frees her to stay on track. This is a way for her to maintain balance and order. Some people feel that when they live by their calendar, it controls them, but Kathy knows that the opposite is true. If Kathy's calendar is full and an opportunity arises, she is in a position of power. She can adjust her priorities to accommodate the opportunity, put the opportunity on hold until she can fit it in, or pass on the opportunity. She is in the driver's seat by retaining continuous involvement in her time-management system.

Those who don't tightly guard their time struggle to keep up with those who do. If you don't know what comes first in your schedule, you cannot recognize and seize opportunities when they arise. If you are in the dark about your commitments, you will constantly find yourself late, surprised, and ill-equipped for the next appointment.

Kathy made an up-front investment when she chose the calendar system she would use at her design firm. She paid good money for the software licenses to use the universal calendar and task-management program in an office-wide network. This way, everyone using the system can see what obligations other staffers have on their calendars. People can schedule meetings around everyone's existing commitments. On her calendar, Kathy assigned colors to each type of activity so she can instantly see when she is out of balance. She consults her calendar practically hourly and works diligently with her assistant and family to stay in sync.

Whether managing your space, time, or finances, your choices will either support or conflict with your priorities. Staying in sync with your priorities requires systems, effort, and self-discipline, as Kathy's life demonstrates. However, the alternative is an existence that is out of control like Mary's life. Mary has never invested in establishing order, and therefore maintenance is out of the question. She is running at full speed but never reaches her goal. She is losing her belongings, papers, time, and self-respect. Mary's disorganization is costing her the ability to live in congruence with her values. This is an awfully stressful way to live! Kathy, on the other hand, has less stress because she works hard to keep her life in check with the things that are important to her. Synchronicity with self is the result of embracing the value and practice of organization.

Act as Your Own Life Manager

Like Mary, many of us feel cheated by our disorganization. We are constantly paying the price for our haphazard lifestyle. In this state of chaos, we are inundated by our burdens and blind to our blessings. If we could change our perspective, we could change our lives.

We aren't organized partly because we have undervalued an orderly life and our own precious resources. Perhaps unconsciously, we haven't perceived our time or our money or our gifts to be very worthwhile, and we have spent them carelessly. Instead of being purposeful about the way we live our lives, we have simply endured our circumstances. Only when we recognize and honor the resources we've received can we start investing in the things that truly matter to us: our life priorities.

If you gave your children a thousand dollars to invest and instead they frittered it away on candy and movies and whatever struck them at the moment, you wouldn't be very impressed. You might wonder where your parenting went wrong! It takes maturity to understand that earning money requires hard work. A realistic understanding of that labor makes investing appealing. Once you appreciate the cost of something, you want to invest it to preserve its value. Like children, we sometimes underestimate the value of our own resources and waste them as a result. Rather than managing our life resources, we can squander them.

We don't often think about the brevity of life and realize that our days on earth are numbered. Instead, we get caught up in a frantic pace and discount the value of our time. As a result, we fritter our time away on activities that steal our energy and don't contribute to our quality of life. People with terminal diseases come face-to-face with the preciousness of life. If they've been living a lifestyle of wasted time, their disease immediately changes their perspective, and they begin investing their time rather than spending it. If we could change our perspective and realize that tomorrow might just be our last day, we would be more likely to invest our time in meaningful ways.

We also undervalue our financial resources. Rather than considering how hard we worked to earn our living, we undermine the value of our money by spending it on useless things. We accumulate for the sake of accumulation. We have so much excess stuff that we have to retain storage units to keep all of it! We have so many things that we actually lose our belongings in our pile of stuff! If we truly understood the value of our money and aligned our spending with our values, we might choose to spend our money differently. In order to honor our priorities, we might invest in experiences and in relationships instead of buying more stuff.

At the end of our life all our money and possessions and clothes will go to someone else. All our labor and the stuff we have to show for it will vanish. The money and the stuff we call ours is really not ours in the long run. It is under our care for now, but it is only ours for a short while. Our assets are blessings that are here today but could be gone tomorrow. If we sincerely believed that every day and every dollar are gifts, we would radically change our behavior.

Time and money are not our only resources; God has also entrusted our talents and skills and relationships to us as resources. We did not receive our mental and physical abilities accidentally; God intends for us to use them for a purpose. Certain people are also in our lives for a reason; we can reach out to them or ignore them. Focusing on ourselves is easy when we are not practicing an awareness of our resources and blessings. When we carelessly use our resources, we act as if we are entitled to them instead of grateful for them. We can mindlessly spend the resources we've been given, or as conscientious managers we can mindfully invest them.

We can stop living recklessly by taking back control of our lives. We need a transformed perspective before we can transform our behavior. If you find that your life has spun out of control and you're surrounded by chaos, you may have been an absent manager of your own life. Things are about to change! I invite you to take on a new role in your life: Become a diligent overseer. An overseer does not feel entitled to what she manages. She recognizes that the belongings and money and time and resources that surround her are simply under her care temporarily. She administrates those resources wisely because she knows they are gifts and not in endless supply. When we comprehend and treasure our resources, we are inclined to treat them with care and manage them responsibly.

If you want to reclaim your life and bring order out of chaos, you can begin a rewarding, freeing adventure! This book is for those who want to order not only their space and their time but their priorities as well. By the end of this book, you will be equipped to bring your daily life into alignment with your priorities. If you put these ideas into action, you can have more freedom and a higher quality of life. Not only will you learn organizing truths, principles, and strategies, you will learn how to become your own life manager!

2

The Disorder Debt

Do you know the feeling of drowning in debt? Of being harassed by your own guilt? Frustrated that you can't seem to get ahead of the growing balance? Scared for your future? Believe it or not, many people describe their feelings of disorganization in the same terms. From anxiety to shame, the emotions that the messy masses experience are similar to those that people in debt endure. Perhaps because disorder is so pervasive and stifling, it evokes the same avoidance and fear that debt induces.

If you relate to your disorder like a person in debt, you may hide from it, lie about it, cover it up, ignore it, and get discouraged about it. Instead of dealing with the piles, you push them aside to make room at the kitchen table or on your bed. You pretend not to see the piles and continue operating within a clogged, unproductive environment. Instead of taking the time to find and pay unpaid bills, you pay the late fee month after month and conceal the consequences. You feel badly that you can't seem to get a grip on the piles and the bills, and your anxiety about disorganization is plaguing you. Like debt, disorganization affects you, your family, and your lifestyle. It forces you into a reactive, fearful role.

Continuing in disorganization is like continuing in debt: You keep getting further and further in the hole. You may simply need to pay off a little debt of disorganization. In this book you will learn an authentic organizing process and some key principles and strategies to do just that. On the other hand, like serious debtors who need a consumer counseling service to bail them out, you may need someone to come to your rescue. I'm standing at the edge of the hole you're in, and I'm tossing you a rope to help you climb out. I hope this book can be a lifeline for you.

Your Coping Strategies

If you have reached a significant point of pain, you may have tried to get organized in the past. Perhaps you've tried to pay down your disorganizational debt by making fervent efforts to dig out. If your strategies haven't worked, and the balance of your backlog keeps growing, you may feel frustrated and even hopeless. Perhaps your organizing endeavors haven't been effective because you have been approaching your problems the wrong way. If you have been haphazardly applying quick tips to your troubles, you've probably only made an imperceptible dent in your disorganization.

The Balance Transfer

We don't like to acknowledge the depth of our debt. Rather than assessing the whole balance and what we will have to do to pay it down, we try to short-circuit the process. To support our denial of the situation, we will try just about anything to find a shortcut. One of our coping methods is to transfer balances.

When your balance on one credit card is increasing and another card offers a lower interest rate, you may transfer the balance to the lower-rate card. You feel relief because you feel as if you've done something to solve your own problem. You've taken action! You've even saved money!

Unfortunately, however, when we examine the logic behind transferring balances, it falls apart. Actually, you've taken your time making calls that will result in more paperwork. You will still have to close your old account and request a letter confirming its closing. You might have missed the fact that the new low-rate card only offers the low rate for a fleeting introductory period. You may well have wasted your time. Don't forget you will have to set up a new file for the new account, cut up your old card(s), and track all the incoming paperwork. Say this process took you several hours over a period of days. If you had spent that time working, you would have gained more funds to put toward the actual debt! I'm not saying that you should never transfer balances in your accounts. I am simply pointing out that transferring balances is an activity that takes time and energy away from addressing the real problem: your balance!

We do the very same thing with our disorganization. Instead of assessing and tackling our disorganization as a whole, we make random attempts to relocate the balance of it. We tidy up one room and shift the contents to another room. We buy more plastic products to contain our stuff rather than eliminating our excess. We overcommit our time because we want to do it all, and then we dodge the very commitments we've made, replacing them with new activities. We cope by shifting around our disorganization. Until we become ready to eliminate our balance of disorganization, we will live in a never-ending cycle of frustration.

The Deferred Payment

A truck seems to appear every week in my neighborhood, delivering brand-new furniture to someone. The truck is a moving advertisement, and its signage offers no payments for two years. Of course, we all know the deferred-payment psychology works on the American consumer, and that includes people in my neighborhood. I would feel weird using and enjoying furniture I hadn't paid for yet. Twenty-four months is a long time. When the time came for me to pay for the furniture I had been borrowing, it would probably have some wear and tear and be much less dazzling than it was when I bought it. By then, I would feel depressed to have to pay off furniture I wasn't even excited about anymore.

Let's look at how the deferred-payment mentality applies to organizing. Suppose you have put off organizing your office for the last few years. You have relegated organizing to the bottom of your to-do list, discounting its importance. Staying late for a few days or coming in on the weekend to organize your space just doesn't seem fair. You figure that you don't get paid to do housekeeping, and you'll get to it later. However, you're starting to get uneasy as the piles have been mounting, and you're working harder and harder to find things, stay on task, and feel good about your work.

Economic conditions have adversely affected your company, and now your boss is looking to tighten the belt. No one is safe from layoffs. Looking around, you notice that everyone else has a fairly organized office and is able to maintain the appearance of being a contributing team member. Suddenly, you realize that your head will be on the chopping block because your disorder has prevented you from contributing at the same level. All this time, you thought you were deferring the pain of taking time to organize, when in fact you were just accruing the pain for later. Sadly, the pain of a layoff is in the end much worse than spending 12 or 15 hours to organize your office.

To cope with our disorganization, we try to defer the pain of facing it as long as we can. Some call it procrastination, but those on the deferred payment plan may call it self-preservation! Unfortunately, our perceived self-preservation may eventually be our demise. Consciously or subconsciously, we are trading taking action for an immediate gratification of some kind. But if we do experience any immediate gratification, it quickly fades. As with the office organizing project, even though we know we are delaying taking action, we often don't experience much gratification in exchange for our delay. We simply hurt ourselves by deferring the problem.

The Interest-Only Payment

Another debt trap we fall into is the interest-only payment. It is deceiving because we feel as if we are doing something useful by making a payment when in fact we are doing nothing to affect the principal. If we miraculously have the self-control to stop spending, then the principal will remain static. Even with a static principal, we will never eliminate our debt by making interest-only payments. In fact, we will be lining the pockets of the lender. The reason the credit card companies are thriving is because lots of people pay more in interest over the life of the credit loan than they ever had in principal! Realistically, though, we will likely keep spending, and our principal will grow. Our interest payments will get bigger as the principal gets bigger. Only by chipping away at our principal will we ever get out of debt.

In the same manner that some people make interest-only payments towards their debts, people often make token attempts to deal with their disorganization. They do the absolute minimum to maintain their sanity. Instead of addressing and organizing their clutter, they stash it in junk drawers, closets, and the garage. They just want to keep their heads above water as they tread furiously to stay afloat. The interest-only organizing approach simply puts out fires rather than dealing with the root causes of the problem.

Disorganization Is a Liability

Debt adds serious liabilities to our lives, and disorganization does too. These liabilities can begin to outweigh our assets. People who are dealing with disorder in their lives feel out of balance. They are burdened by the liability of disorganization they have accrued. Like people in debt, they wonder how they are ever going to make enough deposits of order to reduce their liability and increase their assets.

Being disorganized is in fact a liability to your life. Hundreds of clients over the years have reported to us the distressing outcomes of living with disorganization. In addition to wasting their resources, they experience the pain of living with anxiety, gridlock, confusion, and separation.

Anxiety

Anxiety is a big problem in America. We all know that kids and adults alike are being medicated for anxiety. On-the-job stress causes health problems and costs employers a lot of money in sick time and unproductive employees. Our disorganization is a liability for us because we are mired in anxiety about it. Certainly, getting organized is not the only answer to address anxiety. It is, however, an important step in reducing self-induced stress.

When I began as a professional organizer, I expected people to tell me about their problems with paper, space, and time management. I anticipated that they would share their frustrations about living in a tiny house or coping with ineffective systems. I did not expect that from my very first client appointment, people would pour out their personal and professional problems when I led them through my assessment process. I heard about marriage relationships wrought with conflict due to household chaos. People described working environments and relationships that were strained by their disorganization. Evidently we don't compartmentalize our organizing problems; we experience those problems in the context of an out-of-control life.

My heart broke time after time as I sat across the desk from people who tensely confessed to me, "Vicki, I just want some peace of mind!" I clearly saw that our state of order is intrinsically related to our stress level and our quality of life. Disorganization affects our well-being.

I also saw that my job was not only to implement new systems and fix broken systems for my clients but also to repair their quality of life. I knew that my clients could not begin to reclaim their lives until we put their environment and time in order, which would release them from the liability of anxiety.

Certainly, a simplified environment and schedule will reduce our anxiety, but we need more than that. We need to become equipped to deal with our lives. We can't achieve orderly living merely by hiring someone to simplify our spaces and help us choose good calendar systems, though those are good ways to start. Living an organized life requires that you have internalized your own values and priorities and that you make daily choices to live according to them. Even with an organized space, we will continue to experience anxiety until we align our choices with our priorities.

Authentic organizing should prepare you with tools to prioritize projects, categorize tasks and belongings, and make decisions. In a good organizing process, you should learn how to ask the right questions about your space, take an objective viewpoint, and exercise the discipline of maintenance. Organization is more than simplifying; it is a skill set that equips you for productive living.

Gridlock

Another comment I have heard repeatedly over the years is that people feel stuck and trapped by their disorganization. You probably know the frustration of being stuck in a terrible traffic jam. You can't see the problem, and you have places you are supposed to be, yet you're stuck in a mess you can't get out of. This is a good description of how those in disorder feel. Disorganization produces gridlock in your life. Have you ever been in a traffic jam and wished that your car could hover out of the mess and fly above the tangled traffic? Well, we wish for the same thing in disorganization; we want a magic transport out of the gridlock.

Like a traffic snarl, disorder can cause us to come to a complete standstill and trigger some unpleasant emotional responses. We may get stressed about our mess, but our reaction is entirely unproductive. Wish as we might, we cannot magically extricate ourselves from disorder. As frustrated as we may be, our only viable option is to go through the pain to get to the other side of the blockage. Even as we make the decision to get organized and commit to progress, we may only inch along at first. We need to get prepared with energy and resources for the journey. Eventually, though, we will pick up momentum and break through to the other side of the congestion.

Imagine spending every day of your life in a traffic jam. This is what you are doing if you are disorganized and haven't taken action. Disorder slows our productivity to a grinding halt, or a painful crawl at best. It causes our blood pressure to climb. It clogs up our life with senseless gridlock.

The good news is that unlike a real traffic jam, we have control over our disorganization. We can eliminate the liability of disorganization in our lives by dealing with our blockage and doing whatever is necessary to eliminate it. By discovering and resolving the causes of the clogs, you can break through to the other side. This book will help you identify and remove those clogs.

Confusion

Disorganization produces confusion of all kinds that burdens our minds and hearts. When our homes are piled high with clutter or our desks are buried under paperwork, we are confused and unfocused. When we can't focus, we don't know what to do next. Other people's expectations seem increasingly unreasonable as we wallow in our confusion.

Disorganization causes confusion in our priorities and choices. You may be confused about whether you should provide for your family by working more, or spend quality time with them. Many people wonder how they can successfully do both. You may be confused about whether you should choose to build your business or go back to school. We have many choices to make, and evaluating the opportunities that come our way is difficult if we don't have a solid foundation of priorities. If confusion about your priorities is an issue for you, chapter 6, "The Priority Principle," will help you identify and audit your priorities.

Disorganized people are also often confused about their roles. Many moms who do the shopping, cooking, kid raising, record keeping, cleaning, and household management underestimate the multiplicity of their roles. Many of them report that they feel undervalued and overworked. I agree with them! I tell them that they are the COOs of their household—the chief operating officers. I can see their pride and confidence develop as they begin to internalize and own their newly defined role of chief operating officer. Instead of viewing their variety of tasks as thankless chores, they begin to perceive themselves in a key management position.

As moms understand the significance of their role in business terms, they recognize the important functions they fulfill. They want to learn and practice streamlining methods to simplify their position. Clarifying their role doesn't decrease the responsibilities they carry, but it does eliminate their confusion about their tasks.

When you define your role, you begin to name the categories of work that you execute. You begin to see the scope of your various roles and realize that one person can't do it all. Moms can follow this model at home. They can start by reallocating resources within the "company." They can approach their husbands and enlist their help. If they can't or won't help, moms can approach the rest of their "staff." Moms can teach age-appropriate cleaning skills to their children so that they no longer have to act as the entire family's janitorial service. If the staff can't cover the janitorial role, Mom can hire a cleaning service if she doesn't have the time or desire to clean. Alternatively, if the family can't afford to hire cleaning help, Mom can swap services with a friend.

A mom's role as chief operating officer doesn't require her to actually do the hands-on work of each of her departments; she just ensures their efficient operation. The point is that Mom does not have to be responsible for all the roles within the home, and as the chief operating officer, she is empowered with the right to outsource. If you need more clarity about your roles, see chapter 5, "The Freedom Factor."

If we take the time to reflect, many of us would agree that we're somewhat confused about our priorities and our roles. We know that we are being unproductive and that our disorganization is a liability to our lives. Our confusion can paralyze us from acting on our own behalf. When we don't have a compass of priorities, we are perplexed about our direction and next steps. When we don't understand our role in life, we either drown while trying to do it all or we jump ship to avoid responsibility altogether. The solution is to discover our priorities and roles. The clarity and understanding that come with these discoveries will eliminate your confusion and help you begin to reclaim your life!

Separation

Perhaps the most distressing liability I see among disorganized people is their tendency to separate themselves because of their disorganization. When we are living with personal or professional chaos, we turn inward. Whether we feel overwhelmed, defensive, ashamed, or something else, we retreat.

Consciously or subconsciously, people who are drowning in disorganization separate from others. They fight with their spouses and bosses and kids, and they often withdraw. Their mess inadvertently tells others to stay away. They stop having people over for dinner. They shut their door to their office. They work longer hours to get ahead. Closed off from others, the desperately disorganized try to cope with their frustrations alone. When we are disorganized, our relationships suffer, and we sometimes slip into the trap of separation.

Disorganization causes anarchy in our life. When we are not practicing good self-government, anarchy ensues. Chaos surrounds us, and we feel like a city under siege. When we have the perception that we are under attack, what do we do? We turn inward. We batten down the hatches. We flee from our troubles. We lock ourselves in our tower and wait for a hero to rescue us. The problem is, we're not living in a fairy tale world and we don't really need a hero to bail us out. We must become our own hero.

If you are living with these costs of disorder, you are living with liability. Your disorganization may have already caused you anxiety, gridlock, confusion, and separation. Just like carrying debt, you are paying an inflated price for your disorganization. If you want to eliminate these liabilities and needless burdens on your life, you can do so, but not without effort.

Disorganization Reduction Strategies

Any credit counselor will tell you that getting out of debt will be a process. It won't happen overnight or without effort. You will need to commit to the outcome and accept that the payoff for your efforts will come in time. Immediate gratification is not going to happen. You'll need to address the contributing causes of your debt, your current position, and your prevention strategies for the future.

Those who truly want to get out of debt often cut up their credit cards. In a very practical way, this act severs their access to creating more debt. It is also a symbolic act that indicates a desire to end their bad habits of spending above their means. In similar fashion, you will want to eliminate that which contributes to your disorganization. No, this does not mean that you can ditch your husband or your kids if they are part of the problem! Even if other people contribute to the mess you face, you only have control of your own choices. To change your ways, you will need to change how you think and act about your disorganization.

Change Your Thinking

Many of us have faulty thinking about disorganization. We think that a quick tip will work. We believe that our mess is someone else's fault. We think that if we ignore it, the mess will go away. Examining our thinking is difficult; focusing on our space is easier. If we can fix our space, we figure, then everything will look better, and we will feel better. However, our thinking is the basis for our actions. If we haven't taken action yet, and our chaos is getting worse, then we must examine our thinking to figure out why.

If we believe that we can and should do it all, for example, we will run ourselves ragged trying to be everything to everyone. No organizing process or product could remedy that problem. Until we desire a balanced life more than superhero status, we will probably continue taking on too much and feeling overwhelmed all the time.

If we believe that our belongings are the measure of our worth, then purging our homes of excess belongings will be futile. Just when we dump the superfluous stuff, we may begin to feel our worth sliding and may go purchase more stuff to feel good again. In other words, our thinking drives our behavior, and if we keep repeating self-defeating behavior, we should examine our thinking. Organizing can bring freedom but only to those whose self-awareness makes change possible.

As you read this book, I invite you to consider any faulty thinking about organizing that you might have picked up. Instead of looking for tips you can apply, look for the root causes behind your disorder. Habits are like weeds—if you don't get the root, the weed will return. Typical organizing efforts just slice the foliage off the weed, leaving the topless root behind. Weeds are perniciously relentless, though, and they always come back. Authentic organizing digs down deep and yanks out the whole root of disorder, which starts with our thinking. As you pull a deeply rooted weed, you will dislodge its threadlike runners from the places where they have taken a grip. Slowly but surely, your organizational weeding efforts will begin to free up the soil of your life for productive and orderly living.

Change Your Behavior

Of course, we must also change our behavior if we want to be free from disorganization. Very possibly, we have developed some bad habits that have contributed to our backlog. If you have a serious shopping problem, for example, you will need to not only stop accumulating but also take preventative action. Like the people cutting up their credit cards, you will need to implement some form of self-control in order to stop bringing more stuff into the household.

In addition to eliminating our bad habits, we will likely need to take on some new habits to create and sustain order. If you are working to overcome a messy office, for example, you will not only need systems to manage the paper, *you* will need to manage the paper! You may need to spend a half an hour at the beginning and end of each day to process incoming paper, prioritize it for action, and organize your workflow. Disciplining ourselves with new habits will empower us to sustain the order that we have worked so hard to create.

To pay down your debt of disorganization, I recommend you take the step of scheduling time to work on your organizing challenges. Schedule time to read this book cover to cover so you can absorb organizing truths and principles before you begin wildly throwing your stuff around or preemptively making color-coded files. Set aside some time to apply the methods in part 3: Organizing Strategies. Decide whether you need to proceed on your organizing journey alone or with a friend or expert.

My advice is to hold off beginning your physical organizing process until you've finished the book and gathered whatever support and resources you need. For now, the first step of your payment plan consists of learning, maybe for the first time, about authentic organizing. After you're done reading the book, your next step will entail setting aside blocks of time to execute the methods you've learned with an approach that fits your work style.

I want to encourage you: Getting organized is in fact possible. I have seen hundreds of people radically improve their environment, their use of time, and their quality of life. I've watched souls who are in the darkness of disorder turn a corner and walk into the light of order. I invite you on a journey to understand the causes of your disorganization and learn revolutionary methods for sustainable change.

3

The Disorder Disease

Why am I so disorganized? Isn't that the million-dollar question? If we knew what caused our disorganization, wouldn't we just deal with it and move on? I wish it were that easy! I've learned in my career as a professional organizer that people become disorganized in many ways and for many reasons.

How Did I Get Here?

Figuring out how you became disorganized is like checking your medical history. Your medical records will show when you broke your arm, had an asthma attack, or suffered an allergic reaction. Your records will signify how often you visit the doctor. Frequent visits over a certain period of time may have indicated tremendous stress that affected your health. If you have a new development in your physical condition, your medical records are likely to offer some background and insight into what may be causing your ailments.

To learn about your disorganization, you can check your history. I've observed several means by which people arrive in their state of chaos. Sometimes a precipitating event, like a death in the family or a divorce, can cause disorder. Other times, bad habits are to blame. Each of us had an example to follow in our homes growing up, and we have all been affected in some way by that example. Some of us have accepted cultural norms and have collected our way into chaos. A small percentage of folks have struggled with disorganization their whole lives.

We should note that some medical issues can allow disorganization to creep into our lives. Medical disorders of a depressive, personality, memory, attention, or cognitive nature may be at the core of our disorganization. If you believe that an actual medical disorder is the cause of your disorganization, I encourage you to seek medical assistance.

Most of us, however, come by our disorganization in other ways. To better understand the unique varieties of disorganization, I have observed and interviewed hundreds of people on the topic of how they became disorganized. I'm not a psychologist, but I have discovered at least five basic means by which people have become disorganized. Our life becomes disorderly due to our situation, habits, family history, social behavior, and chronic issues.

Situational Disorganization

Sometimes our circumstances just get the best of us. At work and at home we encounter situations that invite disorder. Things might be going along fine, and then all of a sudden we are inundated by some event or project. When something happens that we did not anticipate or did not prepare for, we can find ourselves the victim of our circumstances. Many people have told me that by nature they are very organized, but unexpected disorder has arrived. These folks are what I call situationally disorganized.

If you have been given a big project with a tight deadline at work, you may have to drop lots of requests until you meet the deadline. Your e-mails and phone messages may stack up in the interim. When you've met your deadline, you would like to feel relief, but instead you have to face a mountain of work that you were forced to let slide. When you have to pick up the pieces you let fall during crunch time, you are dealing with situational disorganization.

Personal loss is another catalyst for situational disorganization that can cause major problems in your household. When a loved one dies, chaos ensues. Life comes to a screeching halt when we are faced with grief. We often cannot cope with our daily responsibilities. The death, the funeral, the obituary, and the probate process all bring unthinkable tasks that weigh heavily on our shoulders. During this time, even rote tasks like dealing with dishes and laundry seem insurmountable. As a result, household order quickly spins out of control. If you inherit belongings, your garage and storage spaces will be flooded with stuff until you have the time to sort through the items and make decisions. All these contributing factors add up to disorder in your life when someone close to you dies.

Many folks I've worked with have not yet lost a loved one but are managing the affairs of an elderly, ailing relative. Sometimes the relative has come into the home or has downsized into a facility. Either way, the responsible party has to absorb all the tasks associated with relocating their loved one into an appropriate location. From the real estate transaction to the estate sale, the person in charge takes on a myriad of tasks.

Those facing a divorce also experience grief and loss. Divorce is a lonely, painful experience that also precipitates disorder in the home. The people involved must make an inventory of household goods. They must report and prove all joint assets, liabilities, and accounts. All this is to determine net worth so that a distribution of property may take place. People in divorce must make provisions for the welfare and future of children and pets. Court appearances and legal paperwork are involved. People dig through their paperwork to answer the required questions, leaving a big mess behind. These unpleasant tasks and the grief that goes with them can paralyze even the most organized. Divorce has caused many of our clients to become disorganized.

Other precipitating events might cause you to become situationally disorganized in your personal and professional worlds. A child graduating and flying the coop might cause emotional overload and temporary disorganization. Experiencing a health emergency or having an accident could cause chaos. Getting a pet, taking an extended vacation, or any unusual life event could cause your tasks and space to collect backlog. Situational disorganization may be caused by a variety of sources, but it can be temporary.

If you can recognize these or other reasons that you have become disorganized, you are taking the first step to restoring order. Knowing that a precipitating event caused your disorder takes a lot of the pressure off you. Many people look around at their clutter and feel ashamed. They wonder why they can't get it together. When I meet people who have been through a divorce, death, or other serious life change, I want to help them see that the disorder that surrounds them is not their fault! They can dig out of their situational disorganization and reclaim their lives.

Habitual Disorganization

Some of the clients I've worked with have needed help redirecting their behavior. Some are stashers. Some are stackers. Others are pilers, spreaders, stuffers, and hiders. You name it, I've seen it. There are a million bad organizing habits, and we've all indulged in some of them from time to time.

Instead of unloading the dishwasher, we leave our dishes in the sink, hoping someone else will unload. Rather than facing the paper pileup, we shut our office door so we can't see the mess. We knowingly overbook our schedule because we can't say no. We resist using a calendar, and important events and appointments fall through the cracks. We all have our own unique collection of bad habits that lead to disorganization. We are the habitually disorganized.

Being habitually disorganized does not mean that we are forever cursed and stuck with chaos in our lives. Rather, it means that we have created our own state of disorganization with our collection of bad habits. Whether we are dealing with space, time, paper, information, or tasks, we all have our own set of patterns that may sabotage our order. We must decide whether we will continue our bad habits and remain in our chaos.

Are you a task dodger? Whether you're putting off a backlog of laundry, yard work, or paperwork, you must learn how to break the habit of procrastination in order to live an ordered life. Do you schedule too many events into your life? A family that is always on the go struggles to keep up with chores at home. Both procrastination and overcommitment are popular bad habits!

The good news is that with the help of this book, you can begin to identify any bad habits that you've developed that are contributing to your disorganization. Acknowledging those habits is your first step to restoring order. If you don't identify your bad habits in the process of organizing, your success won't last. Only when you extricate yourself from self-defeating habits will you truly be liberated from disorder.

Historical Disorganization

My friend Nancy grew up in a clean but disorganized home. Her mom is an inspiration to her, a career woman who worked tirelessly at her job. She worked long hours, so the last thing she wanted to do when she got home was to organize. When Nancy was growing up, her mom chose to spend time at Nancy's softball games and swim meets. She knew her priorities and chose wisely, and Nancy always felt supported. Time away from home, however, meant that Nancy's mom had less time and desire to sort papers or arrange the pantry. In fact, Nancy's mom rebelled against organizing the home and preferred to spend her time doing other things.

As a result, the house had lots of junk drawers and mystery cabinets, and Nancy grew up surrounded by disorganization. After school, Nancy would search for a snack in the overcrowded pantry, and everything she sampled was stale. Food in the refrigerator frequently spoiled due to poor planning. Nancy couldn't help with meal preparation or learn culinary skills because only her mother knew where to find things in the kitchen. The kitchen table was piled so high with papers that Nancy couldn't sit there to do her homework. As a result, Nancy relocated her homework activities to the media room and attempted to complete her assignments in front of the television. Nancy did not learn organizing skills at home and adapted her life and work style around the disorder. Disorganization within the home can alter the way we use our space. We behave in unproductive ways when we are faced with disorganization.

Wired for order, Nancy grew up annoyed with the disorganization. She didn't like having to search for things like a notepad or stapler. Nancy vowed that when she grew up, she would never live in a cluttered environment like her family's home. She wanted to acquire skills she didn't learn in her childhood.

Of course, the opposite of Nancy's story is also true. Some of us grew up in impeccable homes where perfectionism reigned supreme. As we enter adulthood, we may rebel against the order we experienced because it was imposed to restrain us instead of release us. You may be someone who grew up in a museum of order. Along with the order came rules, regulations, and restrictions. You may have rebelled as a result.

Instead of rebelling against order, you have another alternative. You associate order with control, authority, and restraint. But if you began to associate order with freedom, peace, and sanity, wouldn't organizing be less threatening and more inviting? If you have rebelled against orderly living in your childhood, I invite you to embrace the positive benefits of order. By changing your perception of order, you can escape your past and begin to experience true peace.

Finally, some of us grew up in a showcase of order, and we embraced it. We loved the orderly lifestyle then, and we love it now. We are organizing junkies! We can't understand why others would knowingly and willingly live in chaos. We bring our organizing skills into our own adult world and adapt them to our unique needs. We recognize that organizing is not a series of regimented activities but a method of discovery that allows us to correct the things that are not working in our environment and time. We know that organizing isn't a strict set of rules; it is a means of liberation! Our family history equipped us with skills that others may lack, and we may simply be reading this book to augment our understanding of organizing.

Whatever your experience with order has been, you likely have responded to that experience in your adult life. You may have embraced or rejected order based upon your history with it. Becoming cognizant of your past experience with order will help you discover where your feelings about organizing have developed. Your feelings about organizing have likely played a role in how you cope with the disorder that imposes itself upon all of us. Now that you're gaining insight into your sources of disorganization, you are becoming equipped to reclaim your life!

Social Disorganization

The other day, I drove past a storage unit near where I live. The sign said: "If you can't find your lawnmower, bring your garage clutter here!" I couldn't believe the message that the sign was sending! It was encouraging readers to ignore their mess by simply relocating it. Instead of dealing with and eliminating the mess, the sign recommended a stashing solution. I almost pulled in and gave the owners a piece of my mind. However, my business name and phone number are on the back of my car, so I decided that might not be a good idea!

The sentiments of that storage unit sign reminded me of the attitude behind the bumper sticker we've probably all seen: "He who dies with the most toys wins." Our culture encourages accumulation. Some of us wear our stuff like a badge of honor. We think that if we have more stuff than others, we are better or smarter or richer. We want to have name-brand stuff so that we can show the world our financial status. We get more and more stuff, yet we are more and more unhappy and stressed. We are the socially disorganized.

Social norms also encourage us to overprogram our lives. Children are as overcommitted as adults these days. I remember when my brother used to have "daily doubles" for soccer during the summer. The month before school started, the teams started meeting twice a day for drills and practices. Now, soccer kids in my neighborhood are working out all summer long. They are even required to practice and play games through Christmas break! Gone are the summers at the pool and holidays at home.

My clients have shared with me how overly scheduled their lives are as well. Many families earn double incomes but never seem to have time or money to invest in their quality of life. Instead of enjoying family camping trips, Dad has to work all weekend to get the promotion. Instead of making cookies with the kids, Mom is trying to get her home-based business off the ground. Work is not the enemy, and I work very hard myself. I am not criticizing working hard. But when parents and children alike are juggling so many pressures, family life suffers. We become disorganized when we give in to the attitude in society that says, "I have to have it all." This attitude can lead us down a slippery slope of overcommitment.

One of the reasons we collect too many belongings and activities is that we have a hard time saying no. If you have been a victim of social pressures, your choices may have resulted in an overloaded schedule and disorderly living.

You can now make a conscious choice to reject the social pressures that surround you and extract yourself from an out-of-control schedule. You will have to practice the feared two-letter word to release yourself from social disorganization. If you can say no and stop accumulating, you will begin to restore order.

Chronic Disorganization

Chronic disorganization is another way people arrive in chaos. This phrase is not a subjective term. In fact, a group of people study an actual condition called "chronic disorganization." If you've ever wondered why none of your efforts to organize yourself have succeeded, you might fall into this category.

If you've tried a number of methods to dig out, only to find yourself in the same place you started, this may be your unique brand of disorganization. According to the National Study Group on Chronic Disorganization (NSGCD), the description of chronic disorganization includes "having a past history of disorganization in which self-help efforts to change have failed, an undermining of current quality of life due to disorganization, and the expectation of future disorganization." If you've been disorganized in the past, have tried to change on your own, and forecast similar unsuccessful results in your future, you may suffer from chronic disorganization.

Some conditions can coexist with chronic disorganization, like depression, attention deficit disorder, or obsessive-compulsive disorder. These conditions and may or may not be present in an individual with chronic disorganization. Such conditions can exacerbate the living and working situation of the individual with chronic disorganization.

The chronically disorganized likely have a home or work space (or both) that is piled high with clutter. Often, they feel helpless to overcome their disorganization. Indeed, chronically disorganized people require more specialized service than those who came by their disorganization by way of situation, habits, family history, or social influence. Chronically disorganized people are not likely to be able to pull themselves out of their circumstances alone.

The important thing to know is that even if you suffer from chronic disorganization, you do not have to be stuck in disorder forever. I encourage people who think they may suffer from chronic disorganization to visit the website of the National Study Group on Chronic Disorganization at www.nsgcd.org. On this website, you can find a referral directory that will help you enlist the help of an expert or investigate other resources.

Prescription for Change

Many people are quick to medicate their ailments. We pop a pill to treat our symptoms rather than try to discover and eliminate the root causes of our disease. We take the same approach to organizing. We reach for quick tips, hoping for an immediate remedy for our symptoms.

In this book, I am prescribing that you address your problems instead of medicating them. I would rather dispense a solid, viable approach to organizing that lasts for a long time than an enticing but temporary fix. You don't need a treatment plan for solving your organizing problems; you need a restoration process! Treatment implies administering or managing your disorganization. Restoration, however, incudes an investigative process that can actually eradicate your disorganization. Treatment agrees to live with the status quo, simply medicating the problem. Restoration transforms you!

Today, a client called me and cancelled the series of appointments she had scheduled. She said she just couldn't take the time to get organized. I could hear the phones ringing off the hook in her office in the background. She sounded upset and panicked. I could tell that she really needed help.

If I had a little prescribing notepad like a doctor, the first prescription I would scribble out for clients like her would be the advice to slow down! The next prescription I would zip off my little notepad would be for intervention, rehabilitation, and maintenance. Wouldn't you be surprised if your doctor wrote you a prescription like that? Don't we all want the latest and greatest magic pill? We would look at our doctor with confusion or annoyance and demand a quicker, better solution. This prescription, however, will allow us to invest in our own recovery.

Intervention

Intervention is the first step of any recovery program. We all face a moment of truth when we ask for help. Either the pain of our organizing problems is so great that we can't ignore it anymore, or we are inspired to change.

The first step in an intervention is an evaluation process. In a hospital, the newly admitted proceed to triage, where their needs are prioritized. The same thing happens in an organizing intervention. An expert organizer who has received an inquiry from a disorganized person will want to know the scope of the problem and will begin assessing where the client's pain is focused. Of course, you can evaluate your own problems, decide which are the most acute, and begin to tackle them.

Rehabilitation

Rehabilitation is not the same thing as treatment. To reclaim your life from the disorder you're experiencing, you need a process of transformation, not a technique. In order to restore health to your environment or your schedule, you will be acting on your own behalf to change your thinking and your behavior. By understanding organizing truths and principles, you can then begin to apply an informed strategy to your disorganization disease. Too many people wildly apply strategy like a magic pill without first gaining the necessary understanding that leads to the cure.

Your rehabilitation can go as quickly or as slowly as you want it to go. You are in the driver's seat, unlike people who really do have an actual disease. You can change your circumstances; you don't have to be victimized by your chaos anymore. Get ready to ramp up your recovery as you delve further into this book. As you absorb the principles I've set forth, one may stand out more to you than others, and that one principle may be the nugget of truth that you needed to hear in order to break through your disorganization disease. A word picture or client story I've shared might shed light on your own reasons behind your disorganization. When that happens, take action! My purpose in writing is to simply share my observations about how you may have become disorganized, the life impact of disorganization, and some proven strategies to change your ways.

Maintenance

Once you've done the hard work of rehabilitation, you will feel so relieved. The liberation that flows in a life of order is priceless. But in any recovery process, we are prone to relapse. Even if we dig out of our chaos and set up good systems, we will likely backslide if we don't have a solid commitment to maintenance.

One benefit of engaging in an organizing *process* rather than simply applying a collection of tips is that you will identify counterproductive behavior. This self-awareness will help prevent relapse. You will become equipped to identify your own habits that cause disorder in the first place. Avoiding relapse begins with taking a viable, lasting approach rather than a quick and dirty shortcut that will only lead to disappointment. Maintenance is a series of choices that protect your investment in organizing.

I've found that true organizing is a lot like therapy. If you've ever been to personal or marital counseling, you know the drill. You don't get to just dump your problems and expect someone else to wave a magic wand. If you are working with a good counselor, you're not allowed to blame your problems on someone else; you have to take personal responsibility. You examine your past and present to understand why you behave the way you do.

Similarly, in order to create lasting change with your organizing efforts, you will first need to understand how you got in this place of disorder. You may have tried a variety of organizing strategies only to find yourself in the same place you started. You may have applied strategies without first understanding the journey that brought you into disorganization. Typical organizing efforts don't last because they overlook the true causes of disorder and focus solely on the environment. To begin and maintain a successful process of organizing, you must understand your history, assess your symptoms, and engage in your own recovery.

4

No Shortcuts to Order

Will protein-loaded nut bars replace a balanced diet? Do chalky low-fat shakes make us a smaller size for life? Intuitively we know that these dieting shortcuts do not yield the same results as healthy nutrition and sensible exercise. Yet, the weight loss industry is a $33 billion per year cash cow, enticing us to cut corners with promises of dazzling results.[1] We try shortcut solutions because we don't want to go through the pain of changing our eating and exercising habits.

Like the diet industry, the organizing industry is stepping up with its own solutions to problems people face. Retail box stores dedicated to organizing products and storage equipment are popping up all over the country. The media is catching on, and national television reality shows like The Learning Channel's *Clean Sweep* and Home and Garden Television's *Mission: Organization* showcase organizing makeovers. (As a regular expert featured on *Mission: Organization,* I think this is great exposure for the industry!) You can't even go through the grocery checkout line without seeing a proliferation of magazines featuring simplifying themes. The organizing industry is young, it's hot, and it's gaining momentum.

Obviously, I'm thrilled by the increased marketplace awareness that organizing is enjoying. However, I have a growing concern that many purveyors in my industry are beginning to follow the diet industry's lead by promoting appealing yet unrealistic quick fixes. These "experts" give overly simplistic advice to clean up, tidy up, and find a home for everything. Headlines in popular magazines peddle tricks to organize in "three simple steps." Stores offer a proliferation of cheap plastic bins, and we consume them in large quantities and throw them at our clutter. We collect these tools and tips, thinking they are the answers to our problems. Our compulsion to cut corners is deeply rooted. We haphazardly apply shortcuts to our painful mess, and we don't understand why we cannot overcome the cycle of disorder.

The media and a collection of product and service companies are simply responding to what consumers want: tools and tips to arm them for their continual battle against disorder. Some great products and ideas are on the market, but if they are not supported by a discovery process, their effectiveness is limited.

The disorganized masses need the same thing that dieters need: a transformation in lifestyle and habits. The organizing industry could do a better job of educating consumers about the need for *process* as well as product, but the organizing process is not universally understood. I don't fault the organizing industry for proffering solutions to the demands they receive. If consumers demand order-in-a-hurry, that's what they will get! But savvy consumers should understand that quick organizing tips, like diet bars and shakes, are just shortcuts to true transformation.

We Love a Shortcut

If the organizing industry, products, and ideas aren't to blame for our shortcutting habits, what is going on? We are responding to the bombardment of low-cost, low-effort remedies without recognizing that they are inferior alternatives to authentic organizing. Like habitual dieters, we would rather have a temporary boost than a true solution. Instead of looking for the remedy, we settle for a counterfeit.

Authentic organizing is not the cheap, distilled version we see in the marketplace. This book is for those who are fed up with that beguiling but disappointing counterfeit version of organizing. If you are ready to reclaim your life, you are reading the right book. In these pages, you will learn the discovery process that leads to sustainable change. You will learn how to restore order.

Virtually every reporter who has ever called me has asked for quick tips for their readers. I had to chuckle recently when I received a request for "tips that people might use to make the organizing process quick and simple and yet provide a dramatic impact." Give me a break! Sure, you can clear your desk by shoving paper piled two feet high into a lovely wicker basket, and you will have applied a "simple and quick tip that will make a dramatic impact." But the question remains: Will you be more organized with this approach? Obviously, the answer is no; you will simply have a pile of papers jammed into a wicker basket.

I'm hoping that deep down, we all have the common sense to know that "simple and quick" rarely leads to transformation! "Simple and quick" feels good. It feels as if we are taking action against the massive mess, but without adequate time, energy, and thought, we can't achieve real change.

Until now, you may not have heard of an alternative to the counterfeit organizing solutions you've been trying. Perhaps you've purchased products to crack your organizing mystery. Maybe you've rearranged your stuff time and time again but to no avail. Sharing a popular viewpoint, perhaps you've mistaken cleaning for organizing. If you are a busy person on the go, maybe you've just stashed your stuff to create an organized appearance. Many of us have tried cookie-cutter solutions by forcing an organizing tip from a book or magazine rather than attempting to discover what works for us. Whatever our tactics have been, we need to admit that they haven't worked so far and are unlikely to work in the future.

Common Organizing Mistakes

The Product Panacea

The organizing industry is big business. A recent *Newsweek* article reports that home-storage products are a $4.36 billion industry "with sales of objects like wire shelving and acrylic Q-tip holders up a prodigious 10 percent a year since 1998."[2] This trend is an indicator that as a culture we are attempting to gain control of our surroundings. We rush to warehouse stores to fill our carts with plastic boxes, bins, and drawers, and we triumphantly return home to throw these products at the problem. We continuously collect organizing products, searching for the latest and greatest. One of my clients recently joked that she single-handedly keeps the local organizing store in business. For all this consumption, you would think we would have found the answer by now if it was out there for sale! The truth is that the answer to your organizing problems is in the process, not the products.

I am not against organizing products, but I don't like the mass-produced plastic stuff that is made from a mold. Plastic collects dust and has plenty of other flaws. It cracks, it breaks, it sags, and it falls apart. Manufacturers use it because it is cheap. You get it cheap because it was practically free to make. Also, a lot of stuff on the market is just plain ugly. It may look good from a distance, but it is shoddy. If you look in the corners, you may find globs of glue and missing paint. Inconsistencies and dents and uneven edges are everywhere on carelessly made products that are shipped out by the truckload.

Frankly, good-looking, durable, customizable products that actually work are nearly impossible to find. For years, I struggled to find products that would be scalable to my clients' needs. I searched every store, website, and catalog I could find, and still I couldn't turn up products that were utilitarian and aesthetically pleasing.

I was inspired to design my own line of hip and retro organizing products, starting with a home office collection. I zeroed in on the products that either don't work or are missing in the marketplace, and I created an alternative for consumers. With the same attention to detail and using the same discovery process I'm recommending in this book, I conceived products that consumers need but can't find. Supported by hands-on experience, product research, and endless focus groups, I've passionately and vigilantly designed each product myself. Products shouldn't just work seamlessly; they should look good, feel good, and sound good!

I believe that the right products can be a wonderful addition to your organizing efforts if you apply them properly. The mistakes we make with products include purchasing them too soon in the process and believing that products alone are the answer. The correct way to use products is to bring them into your organizing project on an as-needed basis.

The right products at the right time have their place in the process of organizing. When I am working with a client on a pantry organization, for example, I want to understand the family's eating habits and favorite foods. In the assessment process, I try to discover all I can about how they use their pantry and what is working and what is not working. I need to know if the family has growing children who need access to a lower shelf as they begin to learn to help themselves to appropriate snacks. Also, I want to know if the family has very young children whose food intake should be tightly governed. As we are removing items from the pantry in the process, I will discuss with the client how often they use each type of food. This is where I learn that the wife likes to bake and the husband does all the cooking. I learn about their morning routine and their breakfast needs. All these clues are important to understand *before* we purchase any product.

In our pantry project, we might decide that snacks should be placed on the very top shelf because the children are too young to choose their own. Snacks come in a variety of boxes and individual packaging, so we might decide that we need a large, lightweight basket to store all the snacks together. This way, an adult can easily remove the basket from the shelf, lower it to a counter, and pluck out the right snacks. Previous to the discovery process, we might have considered smaller bins, but as the project progressed, new information came to light that required a larger basket.

The correct purpose of an organizing product is to meet an established need, not to simply contain stuff. Used independently of a process, products may be attractive and even functional. However, products cannot truly solve problems and help sustain change unless they are partnered with a useful discovery process. We often use products alone to sidestep the process. By containing, storing, stowing, stacking, and labeling our belongings, piles and paper, we feel like we are making progress, but we are only applying a panacea.

The Rearranging Remedy

Sometimes when we are really motivated, we roll up our sleeves and charge into a room with the goal of conquering the clutter. Like a steely-eyed warrior, we attack our space with a vengeance. Fed up with disorganization, we madly begin sorting and purging.

We might begin in the family room by grouping our junk together in piles. We move furniture out of the way and discover lost game pieces and action figures underneath. We don't know what to do with the game pieces and toys, so we put them in a pile. We circle the room de-cluttering and arranging the stuff within it. When we don't know what to do with something, we simply shuffle it to another spot or another room.

At the end of the day, the room may appear as though our hard work paid off. It may look and feel organized, but one crucial step was missing. We never made a decision about which items should be living in the room. We still don't know the purpose of the family room and its intended contents. We neglected to notice that our piles of like items had counterparts in other rooms of the home. Toys are still flung throughout the house. Paperwork still creeps onto any available surface. By gathering our stuff and paper together, we applied the "group like things together" rule. Yet we are painfully aware that our efforts are likely to dissolve because we've been down this road before. We were in the family room performing this same task just a few weeks ago.

Why don't our organizing efforts to pick up, group items, and move things actually result in change? All we've really done with this approach is to apply the "rearranging remedy." Instead of discovering our unique causes of disorganization and the *purposes* of the room, all we've accomplished is to rearrange its contents. When we shortcut the true process of organizing, we blindly reshuffle our stuff until finally we realize that rearranging is an endless, fruitless task.

The Cleaning Cure-All

One of the most common mistakes we make in our quest for an ordered life is to substitute cleaning for organizing.

The hair on my neck stands on end when people confuse cleaning with organizing. They call our company and innocently ask if we can come "clean up" their mess. Organizing shows on television like The Learning Channel's *Clean Sweep* and The Style Channel's *Clean House* only add to the confusion by associating cleaning with organizing. When folks confuse the two, we have to explain that we are not going to show up at their home or office with a bucket and sponge. Rather, we will arrive prepared to untangle their disorder and apply a discovery process to create sustainable change. Once people understand the difference between cleaning and organizing, they can focus on the real change they've been seeking.

Cleaning takes the grime out of your living space. I love coming home to the smell of bleach or Murphy's Oil. I can tell someone has been cleaning! I enjoy disinfected surfaces, dirt-free floors, and sparkling sinks. Cleaning is a maintenance activity that keeps germs at bay. Cleaning makes your space feel livable and inviting. I look forward to cleaning day!

However, cleaning does not tell you what you should do with the clutter. It does not provide a way to discover the purpose of each room and its appropriate contents. It does not help you understand or change your behavior.

The good news is that you can have both an organized *and* a clean home. When a space is organized, it is easier to clean because you can confidently return nomadic items to their appropriate location, and surfaces aren't clogged with clutter. Yet cleaning is no replacement for organizing. Cleaning may bring you short-term relief, but an organizing process will actually liberate you!

The Stashing Solution

Cleaning can actually create clutter. If we need to spray the kitchen counter with cleaner, we must first do something with the piles of paperwork. Since we are on a cleaning kick, we don't want to redirect our energy to sorting the piles of paper, so we just slide the paper into a drawer or bag. We delay dealing with the paper so we can get the cleaning done. We toss bags filled with clutter into the hall closet and stuff loose ends into drawers to make room for cleaning. We have become victims of the stashing solution.

Stashing has given birth to the junk drawer. Our junk drawers are bursting with a collection of odds and ends, receipts, paperwork, and items we are saving "just in case." As this stashing habit becomes ingrained, we create more and more junk drawers. I've been inside homes and offices where nearly every drawer and cabinet is a mystery space.

Stashing also creates what I call "time capsules." Time capsules are bags or boxes filled with stuff that we wanted to hide. Instead of dealing with the contents and putting things away, we applied a temporary fix: the stashing solution. Our countertop clutter, permission slips, unpaid bills, and long-forgotten projects end up in these time capsules, memorializing a frantic moment in time.

One time I visited a client's home and he offered me a glass of water. I was thirsty and gladly accepted. Instead of going to the sink or refrigerator to fill a cup for me, he poured the water from glass jars lined up on the counter. I asked him about his collection of water. He gave me a sheepish look and confessed that the water company turned off his water service. He explained that he had swept his bills into a bag, and now he couldn't find the bag. Not recalling exactly what was in the bag, all he could do was wait out the consequences. His time capsule was buried somewhere in his messy house, and he was paying the price for having stashed his way into chaos.

Unlike stashing, which offers a quick but detrimental fix, organizing forces you to stop, think, and make decisions about where items really belong. Organizing requires planning and space allocation to activities and items. Because it includes making decisions, organizing takes longer than stashing, but it's worth it. By choosing not to just hide clutter that you don't want to deal with, you're making smart choices to create and maintain order. By doing so, you will prevent clutter from accumulating in the future. Organizing also prevents loss of items, which costs you enormous time, stress, and frustration.

The Tidying Trick

Closely related to the cleaning cure-all is the tidying trick. We have all spent some time tidying up our space instead of organizing it. Rather than restoring long-term order, we've created a short-term neat appearance. This organizing mistake is especially easy to make because it feels so productive!

With good intentions, many of us have stayed late at work or come into the office on a weekend to deal with our messy cubicle. We tossed out old, stagnating paperwork and recycled some tattered files. The feeling of purging quickened our pace, and we felt as if we were gaining momentum. We returned ineffective office supplies to the copy room for the supply vultures to devour. We gathered our completed client projects and returned them to the file room. We even sorted through the papers spread all over the desk and squared up the piles. We tidied and tidied until our office looked presentable. Returning home, we felt proud of our progress.

Sadly, within a couple of weeks we found ourselves sitting in a messy cubicle once again, shaking our heads in disbelief. Why does tidying never last very long? If you have not implemented good systems for capturing and processing incoming paper and information, you will be stuck in an endless cycle of tidying. If you have not discovered and eliminated your bad habits, your tidy space will be sabotaged. If you don't understand your priorities, roles, and job description, you may take on too many projects, neglect delegation, or work in your weaknesses instead of your strengths. An authentic organizing process takes all this information into account but the task of tidying ignores it.

Once you have engaged in a viable organizing process and you've done the due diligence of discovery, you will reduce the amount of clutter in your space. Of course, being organized will not eliminate the need to maintain your space with daily and weekly processing. Maintaining an organized space requires your consistent attention. The difference between processing and tidying is that processing uses systems and procedures to move your belongings and paper along toward action and resolution. Tidying, on the other hand, is just a makeshift method of keeping up.

The Cookie Cutter

We so badly want a magic potion for our organizing challenges that we will try almost any solution. The last serious organizing mistake we make is applying a universal tip or method to our mess. This is the cookie-cutter approach to organizing. I have come to believe that no one tip or trick will work for every person. Each person needs and deserves organizing solutions designed with him or her in mind.

Just because open shelves work in your neighbor's garage, for example, doesn't mean they will work in your garage. Perhaps your neighbor needs open access to items but you like to store your gear behind closed doors. You may admire your coworker's color-coded files for managing paper, but his system may not apply to the type of paper you process. Trays may be a better solution than file folders for the kind of paper you manage. Your girlfriend might use a system for household chores that works in her family, but that doesn't necessarily mean that it will work in your family. Her system might cause a rebellion in your household! Good organizing proceeds from good self-observation. Organizing systems that work are customized to the users, not borrowed from conventional wisdom.

We all wear different sizes and have different body types, and we look for attire that fits our type and style. One size rarely fits all. If you've ever been enticed to buy something that either didn't fit or wasn't quite "you," then you know what I'm talking about. Cookie-cutter organizing solutions may seem tempting at the moment, but like an ill-fitting garment, they will end up in the bad idea pile before very long!

Why We Cheat

If buying products, rearranging, cleaning, stashing, tidying, and using cookie-cutter solutions haven't worked for us yet, you would think that we would come to our senses. One would think that with all of our failed self-help efforts, we would eventually make a decision to bail out of our cycle of disorganization. If we've tried again and again to get organized with products and labels and tips, yet none of those solutions endured, the rational approach would be to try something else.

We are in denial about our true problem: We want an easy shortcut more than we want to find the real solution. Until we come to terms with our failed self-help efforts and commit to engaging in an authentic organizing process, we will endlessly circle around and around in the revolving door of disorganization. To learn about the authentic process of organizing, be sure to read chapter 7, "The Process Principle."

Why do we do this to ourselves? Why do we cheat ourselves and settle for cheap counterfeits for true order even when we know they don't work in the long run? We cheat because shortcuts usually offer a payoff. For example, you feel as if you are making progress when you are doing something, so shortcuts make us believe we are taking action. Shortcuts are supposed to be faster, and we like speedy results. We prefer an approach that promises to be swift, not one that is time-consuming.

Shortcuts also give us a sense of control over our unmanageable lives. Living an organized life in "three simple steps" sounds pretty appealing to those of us who are totally overwhelmed. The promise of control is alluring to the disorganized masses.

But these perceived payoffs aren't really payoffs at all. When we take a shortcut, we don't make progress, we don't get to the finish line faster, and we aren't really in control of our disorganization. Our perception that shortcuts offer a winning approach is false.

We all have our own reasons for taking shortcuts. Most of us aren't even consciously aware of our compulsion to cheat ourselves out of true order. If you habitually take shortcuts but are starting to see that your efforts have been in vain, examine your reasons for taking the easy way out.

Are you looking for the path of least resistance? Do you resist investing the time you would need to really dig out of your mess? Are you worried that if you took on an actual process, you might not have the energy or commitment to follow through? Some people fear failure and don't want to get started with an organizing process because they might not see immediate change. They would rather stay disorganized, taking a shortcut here and there but never having to say they tried and failed.

By dissecting your reasons for cheating, you can identify the false payoffs you've perceived, correct your misconceptions, and address your fears. If you want to stop cheating yourself, start by understanding why you've taken shortcuts in the past.

We need to stop cheating so we can start winning! As we learned on the playing field in our youth, winners never cheat and cheaters never win. Ironically, the person taking shortcuts to order will never arrive at a place of order! We cannot outsmart the system as we begin creating and sustaining order.

Due Diligence

The alternative to taking shortcuts, of course, is going the full distance to reach our destination. Dieters who are tired of the ceaseless cycle of weight gain and loss must decide to get off the pills and bars and shakes and everything else they have tried to shortcut the path to healthy living. If they really want to change, they will need to change their eating habits and lifestyle. Good nutrition won't happen in a vacuum, so grocery lists, meal preparation, and exercise habits will need to change. Binges, unhealthy foods, and sedentary lifestyles will have to go. People who want lasting change must adopt a new mind-set and make disciplined choices.

What's more, people who are committed to their health must step out of a known, comfortable place into an unknown, scary place. They may be inspired by possibility, pain, and their own priorities to lose weight and keep it off for good. In this process of transformation, they will convert from being dieters who think about dieting shortcuts to healthy people who think about developing and sustaining their health.

Those of us who have binged on organizing shortcuts also need a transformative change process. We cannot get to our destination of orderly living by throwing products at our problems or stamping out cookie-cutter solutions. Over and over, we've proven to ourselves that cleaning, stashing, tidying, and rearranging don't work. None of the shortcuts we've tried have advanced our organizing cause. We have exhausted our resources. The time has come for us to restore order and reclaim our lives.

So far in this book, you have become aware that disorder is like debt; it plagues your existence. You've learned that disorganization behaves like a disease and requires intervention, rehabilitation, and maintenance. Now, if you're honest with yourself, you are invited to admit that shortcuts are naive attempts to circumvent real issues.

So what do you do now? You have the opportunity to finally get your organizing efforts right. You can stay in the defeating cycle of disorganization, or you can exercise due diligence to understand and correct your problems. Without due diligence, you will continue to try slapdash methods with unsatisfactory results. If you are willing to put in the time to read this book and apply its principles, you can burst out of the revolving door of disorder and into an orderly life.

What separates those who really want to change their disorderly ways and those who simply say they want to change?

Those who are willing to change are teachable and committed. In his book *Leadership Prayers*, Richard Kriegbaum observed, "Most people want progress as long as they do not have to change very much to get it."[3] If you want to be successful in applying the truths, principles, and strategies inside this book, you will need to trade in your misconceptions about organizing and your shortcut methods. In exchange, you will pick up a whole new way of looking at organizing. Through your due diligence, you'll gain insight and become equipped for your organizing journey. Your change process will transform your thinking and your choices!

5

The Freedom Factor

Disorganization enslaves us to an existence of confusion, anxiety, and separation. Our disorder has mastered us. We are stuck in gridlock, and we spend most of our time putting out fires. We have a nagging feeling that some people have found a better way to live, but we aren't lifting our eyes up to the answer. If we manage to address our enslavement at all, we usually only muster up enough conviction and strength to attempt shortcuts out of our slavery. In order to find our way to freedom, we must throw off the shackles of our disorganization.

Disorganization degrades our quality of life. Full of gifts and talents yet languishing under the rule of disorder, we are unable to release our potential. Instead of enjoying the peace of mind that flows in a life of order, our thoughts are fraught with worry and fear. We are entrapped by a haphazard, messy lifestyle, and we're missing out on the fullness of life. As slaves serve their masters, we serve our master of disorganization with our time, money, and energy. Only when we refuse to be mastered any longer can we redirect our resources toward good and fruitful purposes.

If you feel downtrodden by your disorganization, now is the time for you to break free. Will you allow your chaotic environment and schedule to keep you in a prison of frustration forever? Will you continue doing the same things you've always done with unproductive results? Or will you decide that you want to be delivered from the darkness of disorder?

You have the power to break free. Though you are a prisoner of disorder, you can liberate yourself. As you apply what you are learning, change will come. The more change you make, the freer you will become. Though change will be painful at first, it will get progressively easier as you go. Your momentum will propel you forward.

Frederick Douglass, a famous American slave, said, "I have observed this in my experience of slavery, that whenever my condition was improved, instead of increasing my contentment, it only increased my desire to be free, and set me to thinking of plans to gain my freedom."[1] Douglass understood that once the human mind is enlightened with the possibility of freedom, it is no longer satisfied with enslavement. Once we become aware of an alternative to our harried existence, we must not turn away from that consciousness. We either decide to continue living in our jailed state of disorganization or we decide to escape from bondage. If you're tired of being bound by your chaotic life, I invite you to respond to liberty's call and claim your own freedom.

Organization Clarifies

One of the many benefits of implementing order in your life is the clarity and focus that follow. As you engage in an authentic organizing process, you will ascertain your roles in life. Your job description will come into focus, and you will see where you can most effectively invest your energy. Ordering your life also frees up mental space so that you can think clearly and make better choices. Perhaps most importantly, when you live an orderly life, you can focus not only on your physical world but also on your spiritual world. Too often, we starve ourselves of spiritual intake because we are too busy keeping up with the material demands of our life. The payoff of getting organized far exceeds the promise of saving time and money; the true payoff is the liberty of a clarified life of meaning.

Role Clarity

The discovery process of organizing clarifies your personal and professional roles. Observing clues in your space and calendar, you can look at the way you function. Armed with new awareness about the roles you are performing, you can compare your activities to your actual job description. Knowing your active functions will draw attention to your inactive functions as well. If you find a discrepancy between the tasks you are currently doing and the tasks you should be doing, you can make some decisions about your use of time. Gaining awareness of your situation is the first step.

A husband and wife marketing team hired me to create an office that would work for both of them. Their paper management was a major problem. They dreaded the organizing process because they had disparate work styles and needs, but they wanted to make their office hum with efficiency. After engaging them in a discovery process and examining each of their paperwork, I began to see their roles come to light.

Though Gordon's desk was relatively clear, I found that disorder lurked below the surface. Files with handwritten names were shoved in a variety of drawers. The names were written in pencil, indicating that these files were temporary and probably contained leads. A checkbook and a stack of bills were stuffed in an overflowing folder in the file drawer. Stashed in his top desk drawer were a number of thank-you cards that had lost their corresponding envelopes. One thing Gordon had going for him was his disciplined management of electronic information. He maintained a contact management database and was fanatical about entering all conversations and transactions with clients. From his client files, thank-you notes, and database clues, I determined that Gordon was in charge of business development and responsible for landing new clients. The checkbook and bills told me that he was also the financial manager of the business.

As I shared my discoveries with Gordon, he was amazed that I had figured out his roles. He had never taken the time to make a job description. I explained that his collection of paper and information is a record of his life. It is a mirror of the way he is spending his time and energy.

In our process, Gordon began to understand that his paper and information fell naturally into one of the roles of his job description: business developer and chief financial officer. The light switched on for Gordon. He determined that he could toss or delegate any paper that fell outside his primary roles. This clarity quickened his pace, and he began to plow through his backlogged paper with more confidence and less fear.

I then turned my attention to Gordon's wife. Ginny had a rainbow of file folders full of documents, though she wasn't quite sure what the colors meant. Whenever she wanted to make a new file, she just grabbed a new color. In addition to having a variety of file folder types, she had stocked her cabinets with the latest and greatest office supplies. Her files had vendor names and client names on them, and they sat on her desk where she could see them. The folder labels were computer generated. Her phone rang off the hook while I was in the office, and she struggled to not pick up the line.

From her penchant for office supplies and matching labels, I could see that Ginny acted as office manager. She was responsible for everything from purchasing supplies to streamlining the labeling system. The contents of the client and vendor files and the incessant calls told me that she was in charge of client service.

Ginny, like Gordon, was awestruck that with a little investigating I was able to pinpoint her roles within their company. As she weighed her roles of office manager and client service manager out loud, she became reflective. She liked the office management duties because they offered a respite from the daily grind. However, her passion was truly servicing their clients. She loved extending caring customer service to vendors and clients alike, and she enjoyed connecting the two in mutually beneficial relationships.

After Ginny was able to discover and name her roles, she began to prefer one over the other. She saw that she was overloaded with work and could really use some help. Ginny decided to hire a part-time office assistant to perform the tasks of stocking supplies, making labels, and other mundane activities so that she could work in her strengths. Ginny's newfound understanding of her roles gave her increased clarity about the functions she enjoyed performing and those that she could outsource. Her discoveries actually gave her the freedom to invest more purposefully in the company's most valuable resource—their clients.

Once we established that Gordon was in charge of business development and finances, we immediately saw what kind of systems he needed. Working with his natural affinity for electronic systems, we instituted a simple method for tracking business development activities and an online bill-paying system. As we realized that Ginny preferred her client service role over her office manager function, we could implement distinct systems for her and for the new office assistant. We worked with Ginny's partiality for color and hard copy, so we set up a color-coding system that helped define client and vendor categories. By discovering their unique functions within the company, Gordon and Ginny set up their systems around their roles and optimized their time and passions. The job descriptions we created for Gordon, Ginny, and the office assistant were simply a record of their newly clarified roles.

Mental Clarity

As we've discussed in chapter 3, "The Disorder Disease," disorganization can present itself and cloud our minds in many ways. Medical disorders of a depressive, personality, memory, attention, or cognitive nature may be causing our disorganization and blurring our clarity. If a medical condition is causing your disorganization, you should see a healthcare professional. The vast majority of us, however, become disorganized in our space and in our minds for more common reasons like our situation, our habits, our family history, and social influences.

One thing I know from observing and interviewing hundreds of disorganized people is that disorganization clutters your mind. You spend a great deal of time spinning your wheels, confused about the big picture and what you should do next. My experience has proven that our external environment affects our internal environment.

Disorganized people are distracted by their chaos and often mismanage their time, which negatively affects their state of mind. Physical and mental clutter slows their daily functioning and wastes time. They can't find things and operate efficiently. When their mind is disorganized, they are stuck in a reactive mode because they can't seem to get on top of their problem.

On the other hand, organized people are able to put their hands on what they want when they want it. They can get things done faster and optimize their time. Living in a state of order allows them to see things clearly to recognize that which isn't working for them. They can identify and eliminate the garbage in their environment and schedule. As they proactively weed out the garbage, they consciously make more room for the things that really are important to them. Choosing order allows them to get on with the business of living.

I've found that when my office is organized I can walk in and immediately take charge. I have clarity about what to do first, and I am better prepared to handle the onslaught of daily calls, e-mails, and challenges. In the same way, when I've organized my time realistically, I know what I am supposed to do next and allow myself sufficient time to take care of the things that are important to me.

Conversely, if my office or calendar is burdened with superfluous stuff, my peace of mind suffers. I can't slow down and think because I'm stuck frantically batting at all the balls lobbed in my direction. I can't reflect, track things, or plan ahead when I'm disorganized. My mind is too fraught with anxiety about what I should be doing or the things that might be falling through the cracks without my attention. I feel as if I have to run to keep up. Although I'm an organized person, my space and my time can temporarily become heavy laden. Until I set things straight, I can't slow down and regain my mental sanity.

If you will make the investment to get organized, you will find that one of the best rewards is mental clarity. When you are organized, you are unencumbered by mental clutter that plagues your thoughts. An authentic organizing process will help you become aware of your priorities. As you implement systems to help you cope with your social and occupational responsibilities, you will equip yourself for improved functioning and greater success. People who have taken the time to get organized value their investment and, as a result, are alert and watchful to ensure that their investment is protected. Orderly living allows you to be vigilant in maintaining your systems and your life priorities. The freedom of an ordered mind is peace!

Spiritual Clarity

Perhaps the greatest freedom of an ordered life is clarity about what is truly important. When we are disorganized, we focus too much on the present. We get stuck reacting to our circumstances, trapped in a bunker of self-protection. We live by fear instead of by faith. Instead of lifting our eyes up to our purpose in life, we are simply surviving. Chaos in our physical life perpetuates the chaos in our spiritual life. In order to break through to freedom, we need to climb out of our bunker of disorder.

If our calendars are crowded with senseless activity and our homes and offices are stuffed with excess, we don't have the time or energy to nurture our spirit. We don't have the bandwidth to invest in our faith, reflect on who we are, or consider our purpose here on earth. By eliminating the congestion and confusion in our space and time, we can begin to see things more clearly. We gain lucidity about that which is truly meaningful in life. As our thinking becomes clearer, we can align our behavior with our values. Through our choices, we can honor who we really are inside rather than live in constant internal conflict caused by our chaos.

Clearheaded and organized, we can explore our giftedness and our calling in life. Instead of dealing with matters of urgency and survival, we can deal with matters of eternal consequence. We can begin to answer the questions, Why am I here? and How can I serve? Living an organized life releases us to be in control of ourselves so that we can become all we were meant to be. An organized life is a sane, peaceful existence in which we maximize our availability to God and our ministry to others.

An Investment in Your Quality of Life

Is your disorganization compromising your personal and professional life? If it is, you are the only one who can reclaim your quality of life. You don't have to be imprisoned by the past and the way things have always operated.

Disorganization enslaves us to the moment. We are full of anxiety and fear when we wonder what we are missing or what we didn't do that we were supposed to do. We become used to things falling through the cracks and missing out on opportunities. When we're disorganized, we lack clarity and peace of mind.

The good news is that you can make a new life for yourself by escaping the prison of disorder. By investing in creating and sustaining order, you can live a purposeful, congruent, and liberated life. Leave your enslavement behind and cross over into safe territory. On the side of order you will find a higher quality of life.

Purposeful Living

I've noticed that people who are organized seem to be in charge of their lives. They have clarity about what they are supposed to be doing and the role they are fulfilling. They don't have to spend time mired in confusion because they know their values and are actively living out their priorities. They have exercised their power of choice and have directed their own path instead of waiting to be called on. This is not to say that they are in total control of their own destiny; none of us can control some things like death and disease. But organized people are in the driver's seat of their lives and are living purposefully.

In the office environments in which I've consulted, I've noticed that the organized people are the ones who receive promotions and advance in their careers while their disorganized counterparts stand on the sidelines. Why is this? Since their work is turned in on time and is of good quality, organized individuals gain traction within their companies and create a positive reputation for themselves. Because their work is organized and thoroughly researched, their coworkers and managers have confidence that they have done their due diligence.

Organized individuals who have made an investment in order have usually done so intentionally. They understand the connection between their priorities and their choices. They understand that to be the kind of parents or spouses they want to be, they need to be plugged in to their kids and their marriages. This requires them to actively engage, communicate, and be present with their family. In their professional world, they know they will have to perform consistently in order to establish their value within the organization. Since their performance depends upon them having viable systems and processes, they invest in creating and maintaining those systems. Organized people recognize that every choice they make conveys their commitment to their personal and professional priorities.

Congruent Living

I don't know about you, but I experience tremendous anxiety when I am not living in sync with my values. When I have my priorities mixed up, I can spend my time on things that are insignificant in the big picture. This anxiety is constantly with me until I straighten out my priorities and align my choices with my values.

For example, if I spend too much time working and not enough time with my husband, I can feel our relationship suffer. My own choices have compromised my quality of life. Of course, like all businesspeople, I experience times when a big project or deadline monopolizes my focus for a while, but I'm not talking about those special circumstances. I'm referring to my tendency to work too many hours and become a workaholic. When I get into a cycle of ceaseless work, my tunnel vision is not in line with my true priority to build an intimate marriage. Until I shift back into balance, I will be anxious, knowing that my husband is waiting to have some of my time and that I truly want to give it to him.

I am always amazed to see how happy Trevor is when I quit working and we head out to the airport. Flying is his passion, and as a private pilot he loves taking people for tours. I am his favorite copilot, and I cherish the fact that I am his first choice for a passenger. He invites me to go flying from time to time, and too often I tell him that I am in the middle of a project and too busy to go with him.

When I do take the time to plug in to his passion and share in his joy of flight, he lights up. He pats me on the leg while we're up in the air and asks me if I'm having fun. On the drive home, he comments repeatedly how glad he is that I came with him. He softens to me, and our conversations are more connected. When I take the time to fly with Trevor, we become closer. I want to be the kind of wife who doesn't just say she values an intimate marriage but who proves it with her actions. I invest in my own quality of life when I live congruently with my priority to build an intimate marriage.

How can being organized help you to live congruently with your values? An authentic organizing process will help you discover your life priorities. As you examine yourself—as you will have the chance to do in the next chapter—you will hold up a mirror to your personal and professional life.

You will discern whether you have been living according to the things that matter to you or at the whim of the demands of life. To live in congruence with your values requires that you know what those values are. Discovering your priorities can be exposing because, like me, you might find that even though you know what they are, you don't always make choices to honor them. This self-awareness can be a catalyst to put your life in order!

Living in an orderly way keeps us focused on that which is truly important, not distracted by mental and physical clutter. Organizing your space and time is not enough to help you live congruently. Only when you set your priorities before you and determine to live in a manner that honors them will you experience the contentment of living a sane, authentic lifestyle.

Liberated Living

Are you ready to let freedom ring in your life? Before you can truly be emancipated from disorder, you may need to change some things, and change isn't easy. You might get inspired to change by your own priorities and by the possibilities in your life. On the other hand, you may be motivated to remedy your chaotic environment or circumstances out of sheer pain. Because of their disorganization, many people are experiencing the pain of wasted time and resources, the pain of shame, or the pain of missed opportunities. I have written three chapters in this book about the primary catalysts for change: priorities, pain, and possibility. If you want to be liberated from the mess you're in, these principles will help you embrace a transformative change process.

But what if you're not the only one who needs to change? Frequently a woman raises her hand at one of my speaking engagements and asks me, "What do I do with my disorganized husband?" Feeling her pain, I laugh and respond that until her husband is ready for change, she can do very little. Until then, she can set a good example with her own self-discipline. She can model a life of clarity and quality. She can teach her children how to create systems and how to pick up after themselves. I know from personal experience, however, that she cannot expect her husband to change until he is ready. She can encourage, beg, yell, coerce, bribe, cry, and reason, but she won't get very far. Believe me, I know!

Ultimately, we can only control ourselves. Happily, a lot is within our control. All the space that we are in charge of can sparkle with order. Our own personal calendar can be streamlined to support our priorities. We can spend our own time investing in the things that matter to us.

We have to let go of whether doing all the work to make this happen is fair to us. It probably isn't entirely fair, but as my mom has often told me, "Life isn't fair; get used to it." I don't mean to sound cynical about this, but we can only be responsible for changing ourselves. Learning this bittersweet truth has taken me a long time. But as far as it depends upon me, I can arrange my space and time to align with my values, and I can live a life of order and purpose. That is incredibly empowering. I have the freedom to direct my choices; I have free will to live an orderly life. You too have the freedom to claim a life of order.

How does this work in my everyday life? I have to give up the things I cannot or should not control. The garage is my husband's domain. It is chock-full of equipment and tools. From floor to rafter it is bursting with stuff he says he needs. In my biased opinion, our garage ranges between mildly disorganized and horrifyingly disorganized at all times. It can get so bad that I don't like parking my car in the driveway when the garage door is open because my rear window has my business name, Restoring Order, emblazoned on the back! I rue the neighbors witnessing our hypocrisy!

Though I have tried to impress upon Trevor the virtues of putting things back where you got them, this freeing truth has never taken root in the soil of his brain. I've recommended that we group like things together and create storage zones for various kinds of things. I have shared my expert advice that cleaning up as you go can prevent clutter from forming and protect your workspace. He has been immune to all my wisdom. He says he'll get to it later. He is unfazed by my logic or my pleading.

He is not uncaring; he just simply doesn't see the need. He would tell you that his quality of life is peachy, and organizing his garage would not improve his condition. I used to fight with him about it and try all kinds of coercion methods, but now I have accepted that the garage is his domain, and I don't have control over it. This might sound like giving up, but to me it is freedom.

I can be liberated by my own state of order in all the areas I direct. I find that my peace of mind is strongly connected to my state of order. When my office and home are in working order, I feel that I am exercising care over those areas. I enjoy keeping my space and my calendar in sync with my values. It keeps me nimble; I am able to respond to professional opportunities because I am organized. However, I have to recognize that not everyone values order in the same way I do. I have released my husband to live with the state of order that is comfortable for him in his own space. I can even laugh at myself and my vain efforts to control him. My own liberation does not depend on others; it depends on me.

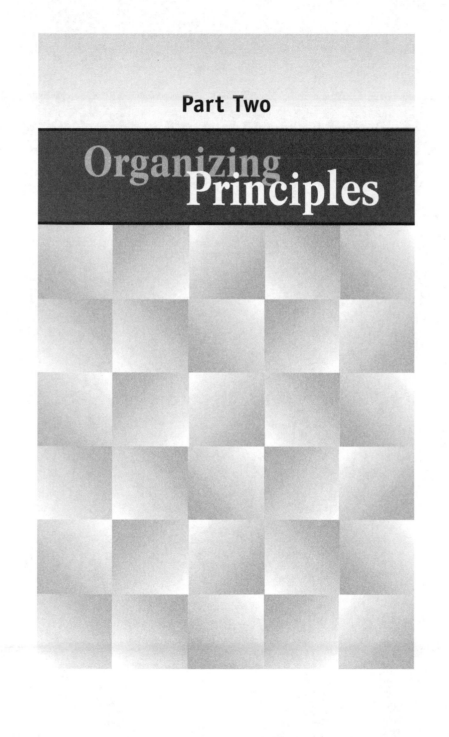

Part Two

Organizing Principles

6

The Priority Principle

Even a professional organizer can become mired in the frustration of disorderly living! When I don't have my day planned and my priorities straight, the moment I sit in front of my computer, my day is hijacked by the pressing demands on my time. I get drawn into the vortex of e-mail, employee requests, ongoing projects, client questions, and constant phone calls. With so much on my plate, I must be purposeful about my priorities and my use of time if I want to accomplish the most important tasks at hand. Often I end up reacting to urgent demands on my time instead of acting on my own behalf. When someone else's priorities seize my day, I don't feel in control anymore. Like a victim of a carjacking, I get pushed out of the driver's seat and find myself a passenger in my own life!

When I am in this reactive mode, I feel as if I'm standing in a batting cage, frantically batting at all the balls someone or something is throwing at me. I don't even get to run for a base because this cage offers no advancement. High-speed balls are coming so fast that all I have the time to do is defend myself. When I step back and evaluate the position I'm in, I realize that I have allowed other people to hijack my daily priorities. I have chosen to respond to other people's demands instead of behaving in my own best interest to do the things that matter most in my day. If you've ever felt like I have, the time has come to reclaim your priorities!

Orderly living requires discipline, so all of us can become derailed on a daily basis if we don't make choices that honor our priorities. If we're not vigilant, other people will define our priorities for us! The Priority Principle is this: To create sustainable order, we must first identify and live according to our true priorities.

What Are Your Priorities?

I ask clients who want to get organized, "What are your priorities?" Many are startled by the question. Almost everyone asks for clarification: "What do you mean, my priorities?" Many believe that organizing your environment is simply about sorting, labeling, storing, and tidying. They've heard that organizing is a controlled process of setting goals and agendas, breaking tasks into manageable parts, and keeping lists. Organizing your space or time may involve some of these strategies, but true organizing is much more. Those who want to order their life in a meaningful way will begin not with strategy but with their priorities—the things that truly matter to them.

I ask those longing for order, "What is important to you? What fills your fuel tank? What do you hate to push to the back burner?" The light of understanding begins to flicker. Some say they want to be good parents, or have more time to play golf with their friends. Others talk about their professional priorities. A few mention that they'd like to have good marriages or develop their spiritual lives.

Our performance-based culture programs many people to begin talking about what they want to achieve with their goals. I share with my clients the difference between a goal and a priority. The terms "goal" and "priority" are often used interchangeably. A goal is finite and measurable, and once you achieve it, you can check it off a list. A priority, however, is an expression of your guiding beliefs and values. Making a certain salary is a goal, but making an indelible contribution to your company is a priority. Attending your child's soccer game is a goal, but being an engaged, attentive parent is a priority. If you live by goals, you may feel as if you are ceaselessly striving, because once one goal is reached, it is invariably replaced by another goal. If you live by your priorities, you can experience contentment.

A Catalyst to Get Organized

A successful organizing process is one that is motivated by something greater than a yearning for tidiness. Most people decide to get organized because being disorganized has negative lifestyle consequences, and they want to eliminate those costs of disorder. If they reflect a little further, however, they will also see that being disorganized is causing them to live in unproductive, unfulfilling ways. Their life priorities are casualties of their chaos.

You may have experienced negative consequences to having too many calendars as important events repeatedly fall through the cracks. You may have a spouse nagging you to manage your time better or to "clean up your act." You may even have a boss who is unhappy with your productivity. All of these circumstances could cause you to reach a point of pain in your life and may trigger you to change. Pain is indeed a motivator, but I have found no motivator to be more powerful and lasting than an individual's own priorities.

Organizing our time and environment will take energy and resources, so we need a reason to justify the effort to get organized. Most of us wouldn't begin the organizing process simply to have a color-coded calendar. However, if getting organized brings a worthy payoff, we will be more likely to engage in the process. If we could recognize that the results of our organizing endeavors enable us to fulfill our priorities, perhaps we would be more willing to go through the effort. Our own priorities can serve as a catalyst for change.

Instead of being motivated by negative consequences, you can be motivated by positive results. Rather than fearing losing your job, you can be inspired by your priority to make a meaningful contribution to your company. Instead of constantly arguing with your spouse about the overstuffed basement, your joint priority to have a harmonious marriage can be a catalyst to tackling that project. Your life priorities can offer enduring inspiration for change. Once you identify and embrace your priorities, you will become motivated to order your life to accommodate those priorities.

Questions to Identify Your Priorities

One of my favorite moments of silence happens in my speaking engagements when I offer my audiences one minute to record one personal and one professional priority. Some quickly begin writing while others stare off into the distance in a pensive mood. All at once, the audience is united in pondering the things that truly matter. The minute usually stretches into two as heads are still bowed over their assignment. An impatient few tap their pens and look at me as if to say, "Let's move on." The majority, however, are engrossed in their task as they welcome a rare opportunity to focus on the guiding priorities of their life.

What Are My Values?

If you want to discover your life priorities, you can start by asking a few basic questions. The first question to ask is this: What are my values? A value is something you hold in esteem, something you deem worthy or important. You might value the Golden Rule—to do unto others as you would have them do unto you. Perhaps you value an intimate marriage, the blessing of parenthood, or practicing charity. Considering our values brings focus to the intangibles rather than the material concerns that consume our attention on a daily basis.

What Are My Responsibilities?

The second question that will help you ascertain your priorities is this: What are my responsibilities? All of us have responsibilities to ourselves, to family, to others, and to work. For example, I have a responsibility to my employees. In simple terms, my role is to generate business. If I do this diligently, each one of them can contribute their talent and collect a paycheck in return. Using the word "responsibility," my priority is to *respond to my ability* in executing my role.

Listing our personal and professional responsibilities is a valuable exercise. Once we become aware of our responsibilities, we are accountable for how we choose to handle them. Our key responsibilities in life should help us form our priorities. Beware of taking on too much outside your key roles, or you might drown in overcommitment. In addition to their family and work, some people overprogram their lives and then mistake those commitments for responsibilities. Your priorities should proceed from your primary responsibilities, not someone else's expectations of you.

What Are My Gifts?

Another question to pose when considering your priorities is this: What are my gifts? We all have natural talents and skills. Living life without knowing your abilities is like driving a car with only limited knowledge of how it works. You can operate a car if you're only familiar with the ignition, steering, gas, and brake, but your enjoyment of the car will be limited. If you are blind to your own capabilities, you cannot prioritize those capabilities. Discovering your aptitudes will allow you to operate at full capacity and enjoy the talents you've received.

You begin to live life to its fullest when you discover and embrace your God-given gifts. As you become aware of the special gifts that you have received, sharing them with others will become a priority for you.

How Do I Want to Be Remembered?

Here is a last thought-provoking question to discern your true priorities: How do I want to be remembered? We easily become distracted by the daily grind and take for granted the gift of life.

People have been pondering the brevity of life for generations. If we could stand outside of ourselves and take an eternal perspective on our life, we would see how brief a lifespan can be, and perhaps we would be more committed to making the most of our time here on earth. The Bible puts it this way: "Man is like a breath; his days are like a fleeting shadow" (Psalm 144:4). If I want to be remembered for my kindness, one of my priorities should be to practice generosity in this life with friends, family, and those less fortunate. If I want to be remembered as a woman of faith, then one of my priorities here and now should be getting to know God and developing my spiritual life. The answers to the question, How do I want to be remembered? will highlight the legacy we hope to leave through living our true priorities.

By examining your values, responsibilities, gifts, and legacy, you can identify your priorities. Once you embrace the significance of your priorities, you will be inspired to order your life to honor those priorities. This is the essence of why we should become more organized: to live in line with our priorities and to maximize our brief stay on earth! Knowing and desiring to honor your priorities with your life is *the* place to begin your organizing process.

Priorities Audit

Two Simple Priorities

I bet a lot of your priorities have to do with people. Human beings need and enjoy community with one another, and that is why we long to build and sustain relationships. You might be surprised to learn that if relationships are your priorities, you share God's priorities!

God values relationships above all else. The Pharisees asked, "'Teacher, which is the greatest commandment in the Law?' Jesus replied: 'Love the Lord your God with all your heart and with all your soul and with all your mind.' This is the first and greatest commandment. And the second is like it: 'Love your neighbor as yourself.' All the Law and the Prophets hang on these two commandments" (Matthew 22:36-40). The two key priorities for humans are to love God and to love each other. It's that simple. God's priorities for us have nothing to do with meeting financial benchmarks, ensuring our kids go to suitable schools, or living in the right neighborhood. He wants us to experience a good relationship with Him and good relationships with others.

How can we make sure our priorities shape our everyday reality? To examine whether something is a priority for you, investigate whether you spend your resources on that priority. Two currencies at our disposal are time and money. We spend our time and finances on the things that we want to spend them on—the things that are important to us. If we don't spend time and money on something, it probably isn't one of our priorities.

Reclaim Your Time

If you would say that being an engaged, active parent is a spiritual priority for you, but quality time with your children does not show up on your calendar, you can question whether it is truly a priority for you. Perhaps you've been squeezing "quality time" in between dinner and homework. Only you will know if your priorities are evident in your use of time.

If you find a disconnect between the priorities you claim and the lifestyle you live, the good news is that you can begin now to audit and change your schedule. Get out your calendar and reclaim your time!

Instead of populating your calendar with all your commitments, meetings, and obligations, begin with a blank calendar and your priorities. If being an active parent is a priority for you, schedule special time with each child on a weekly basis. If your faith is a priority, enter a recurring appointment for church each Sunday. You are the only one who can adjust the way you use your time and to put first things first.

Reclaim Your Finances

The same approach can apply to your finances. If investing in your marriage is a priority for you, you will allocate resources to invest in your marriage. Whether you set money aside for a monthly date night, a weekend getaway, or even a counseling session now and then, investing your finances in your marriage will build a strong foundation.

If reclaiming your finances is a priority for you and you don't know where to start, find a study on financial management and commit to a schedule of learning until you know how to proceed. If you're single and saving for your future is a priority, you might schedule a monthly draw from your checking to a savings account. If you're married, and controlling spending to live within your means is a priority, set some dates with your spouse to establish a family budget. Once it is established, set a monthly or quarterly financial review. Dedicating commitment and action to your priorities is the key to actualizing them.

Aligning our resources with our priorities takes time and maturity. The point is to establish a structure for your use of time and finances to accommodate your priorities. When we vainly hope to fit our priorities into an already crowded schedule or maxed-out spending account, we are fooling ourselves. If we are not purposeful about managing our time and our money, we will be controlled by our overburdened schedule and funds. Some of us cannot live our priorities until we take back our calendars and our finances!

We are being inundated by the superfluous concerns of life, and we are starving for substance. Discovering and scheduling your priorities will prepare your life for practical and spiritual readiness. We've often heard that organization equals space, paper, and time management, but it really is not about *managing* anything. Organizing is about making room in your life for the things that truly matter to you. Organizing is simply creating an environment and lifestyle that honors your priorities.

Discovering True Success

One of the primary complaints I hear from folks who seek organizing help is that they are not enjoying their life or their work. Most are too overwhelmed to do anything but survive. They're going through life hanging on to their sanity by a thread. As we talk through their issues on the phone, I can hear their discontent. They are dissatisfied with life and feel cheated by their chaos. They don't know how to change their situation, and the shortcuts they've tried have failed them. Lacking answers and surrounded by disorder, they hope to find resolution through organization.

As I've worked with disorganized people, I've realized that everyone needs a reference point in life. We need to have a foundation from which we make choices. That reference point is fashioned out of our own life priorities, which are an expression of our values. As you've answered the questions in this chapter and thought about your priorities, you may have found that you've placed an emphasis on the wrong things in life. Only by examining your day-to-day focus will you uncover your actual priorities. You cannot manufacture priorities; all you can do is expose them. You may say that family is a priority to you, but if you work incessantly without dedicating time to your family, your lifestyle will call your commitment to your family into question. Your family may not, after all, be the priority that you claim it is. The priorities you verbalize or aspire to may not be your actual priorities.

Your priorities proceed directly from your definition of success regardless of whether you've ever articulated that definition. Why are we talking about success? Here's why: Your priorities can motivate you to get organized because they define the payoff for all your hard work. You invest the time to get organized so you can enjoy doing the things that mean the most to you. The point of organizing is to make room in your life for the important things. When you are finally prepared to experience a better life, you will probably be disappointed if your priorities lead to a false definition of success.

When you look at how you spend your time, you may find that your actual priority has been to make as much money as possible. You may have unconsciously equated success with financial security. If you are in emotional or spiritual conflict with the priorities you've been actually living, there is hope: You can redefine success and then align your choices with that definition.

When my clients examine their priorities, many of them realize that they don't even want the kind of success they are striving for. What they really want is a simpler life where they can find contentment.

Inspired by their desire to find the meaning of true success, I searched high and low for a definition of success grounded in truth that I could offer them. I investigated famous quotes and poems. I looked to socially accepted definitions and came up empty-handed.

I propose a new...well, actually a very old definition of success that comes from a compilation of a few statements in the Bible. The first is this: "That everyone may eat and drink, and *find satisfaction in all his toil*—this is the gift of God" (Ecclesiastes 3:13). The second is this: "When God gives any man wealth and possessions, and *enables him to enjoy them, to accept his lot and be happy in his work*—this is a gift of God" (Ecclesiastes 5:19). Here's an age-old definition of success that you can count on. Quite simply, we are successful when we find *satisfaction* and *enjoyment* in our relationships and work.

Isn't that a freeing description of success? When I stumbled upon it, I breathed deeply. It was an awakening for me, and I hope it is for you too. My job on earth is not to run as fast as I can on the hamster wheel of life after all. I don't need to make a name for myself or strive to reach a certain benchmark that will prove I succeeded. Success is not about meeting an expectation. I felt relieved when I learned that I could be successful without achieving a litany of goals. I found that I could be successful just by being satisfied with and taking pleasure in my relationships and work. This eye-opener was nothing short of revolutionary for me. It changed my thinking, which in turn changed by behavior.

True success, as it turns out, is about contentment. Finding satisfaction and enjoyment sounds so easy, but I have learned that it requires release. I have to free myself from the limits and expectations I put on myself in order to truly be satisfied with who I am and what I am accomplishing. I have to practice an attitude of thankfulness to really enjoy each day. By nature, I want to perform and achieve. Nothing is wrong with wanting to have something to show for your time and effort or with being a passionate person with a lot of drive. But if we are never satisfied, we should be concerned. I've heard people say that we need to remember we are human beings, not human doings. I have to remind myself of these truths often so that I remember that I can find success in this very moment.

Now, I'm a practical business person, and I'm not advocating that we toss out our concern for measurable progress or deliverables. I'm also not promoting a warm and fuzzy view of success that is intended to make us feel good about ourselves all the time. In business and in life we need to know if we are achieving what we set out to achieve. We need to work hard and be held accountable for our actions. The key is that our success is not determined by an outcome; it is determined by our contentment. Therefore, if our boss rejected the proposal we prepared, our professional success is not destroyed. If our children don't behave properly, our personal success is not annihilated. Many of us have let outcomes define us.

You might be thinking this definition of success is just too feeble. Don't we have to take action to be successful? Indeed we do. Successful people are not passive; they are proactive. They plug into their work and relationships with passion.

They endeavor to enjoy the journey and watch their labor pay off. Success is finding deep satisfaction in the simple things, the things we often overlook or trample on our way to the top.

As I've shared this definition of success with audiences and clients, its impact has astounded me. Some people have become emotionally overwhelmed and even cried when I've shared that all they have to do to find success is to enjoy and be satisfied with their relationships and their work. Their relief, like mine, has been palpable. Their benchmarks and false beliefs have imprisoned them to constant activity. With this new understanding of success, they can approach the organizing process (and in fact their whole life) free from the fear of failure. They can focus instead on a continual growth process.

I am convinced of a spiritual connection between success and freedom. As long as we define success in terms of measurable outcomes, we will always be measuring ourselves and coming up short. As you examine your priorities and search your heart, I invite you to embrace God's definition of success. Read on and step into the freedom of a truly successful life!

7

The Process Principle

Betty called our office on a Wednesday morning in a panic. She was having guests over for dinner on the weekend, she cried, and the week was half gone! She didn't know what she was going to do because her dining room table and kitchen counters were covered with clutter. She couldn't even see the top of the table, so setting it with linens and china was out of the question. How would she prepare food and serve a nice meal? What was she going to do with all that stuff? Betty was calling for emergency help.

We were able to rush over one of our professional organizers to begin digging her out of her mess. Without seeing the space, we couldn't promise that she would be clutter free before the big meal. It's a good thing we didn't promise a miracle makeover because Betty had an iceberg lurking underneath the surface!

Upon arrival, we saw piles of bills and mail. Layers and layers of paper covered the dining room table. Vitamins, medicine, household clutter, knickknacks, and mounds of paper were spread on the kitchen counter. Noting these physical clues, our organizer led Betty through our intake assessment in order to better understand her situation and her needs. How did this happen? What were the contributing factors? Betty obviously did not arrive in this situation overnight, and our organizer wanted to give Betty long-term solutions.

Betty tapped her foot with annoyance and sighed a lot during the assessment, so the organizer abbreviated her interview. Betty said she wanted to "get on with the organizing!" In that brief evaluation, we learned that Betty had been accumulating, saving, procrastinating, and shuffling paper interminably. She undervalued understanding her organizing problems and her own habits. She was willing to settle for the temporary appearance of order.

Betty had stacked, piled, and spread her way into total paper mayhem. While sorting through mail on the table, our organizer noticed collection notices and late-fee bills. She suggested setting up a bill-paying system so that Betty could avoid these penalties. She explained that a bill-paying system would help Betty stop wasting precious funds. Betty resisted and exclaimed that she just wanted to clean up for the weekend dinner.

In the kitchen, our consultant recommended pulling items out of the overstuffed cabinets and organizing the contents so they wouldn't spill out onto the counters. She reminded Betty that stashing the clutter would add to the problem. Betty politely declined, saying she just wanted to hide the clutter for now so that her guests wouldn't see it.

Not surprisingly, after only a few hours chatting and working together, our consultant learned that Betty had hired several organizers before hiring our company, and a clear understanding of the situation began to take shape. Betty was a repeat offender and a crisis maker! Instead of establishing and sticking with systems, she would let things go until they became critical, and then she would hire a professional organizer to come help her dig out.

When she had an expert in her home, Betty would direct the organizer to help her put things out of sight. She treated them as if they were from a cleaning service, not an organizing service. The experts advised Betty that she was in a self-defeating cycle, but she avoided taking the time to set up workable systems. She was trading long-term peace of mind for the short-term appearance of being clean and tidy.

Why did Betty just let things go and wait until a situation became critical? That question is probably best answered by a counselor or therapist! From our perspective, Betty was undervaluing the discovery process of true organizing and would likely never achieve sustainable change without engaging in this breakthrough evaluation.

One of the greatest challenges of my work as a professional organizer is to educate people about what authentic organizing really is and what it is not. Most people think organizing is an end, an outcome. They think they arrive at being organized through activities, which may include sorting, grouping, arranging, and tossing. Those activities are certainly involved in organizing, but if they don't include a useful discovery process, no lasting change can occur.

Getting organized is not simply executing various activities. An authentic organizing process will uncover the reasons behind the disorder and show people their priorities and unique needs. For our efforts to last, we must understand that organizing is a process rather than a goal. Many of us would love to check organizing off our list, but it isn't an objective that we can achieve once and for all. Like healthy eating, living an organized life includes ongoing, disciplined choices.

The Process Principle is this: Organizing is not a set of activities; it is a fluid, natural, revealing process in which you discover solutions that fit with your environment and lifestyle. In this chapter we will see that organizing is a discovery process, an organic process, and a self-awareness process.

The Discovery Process

Forensic Investigation

Trevor and I don't have cable television. We made this choice because we don't have much time for television anyway. So when we travel and stay in hotels, we jump on the bed and click through the channels like preteens. We fight over the remote and are glued to the set. Two things we can agree on are the History Channel and crime shows. We admit we're geeks, and we love to watch shows like *Cold Case* or anything with crime scene investigators, especially when the story really happened. We like to see the bad guy get caught because he had rare sand in his shoes or a telltale hair on his jacket. If you take out the gory part, forensic investigators have a fascinating career. They get to ask questions, observe the details others have missed, read between the lines, let the evidence tell the story, and ultimately solve crimes and mysteries.

Recently, I was trying to describe to someone how my team of organizers works to solve paper problems for our clients. I was describing the way we deal with paper flow and systems and how we go through every single piece of paper in an office to get to the bottom of the barrel. We leave no paper unturned. We empty the room. "I guess we do forensic paperwork!" I exclaimed.

We train our organizing consultants to ask questions that will help our clients discover their priorities for their life and space. Once we know our clients' priorities, we can build systems for their time and paper and environment that support the lifestyle they desire. People who want to get and stay organized will explore their causes of disorder. For more on discovering your unique causes of disorder, refer back to part 1: Organizing Truths. People committed to order will continue asking themselves questions as they progress in their organizing process.

For example, if you're beginning to tackle your kitchen and you notice that papers are accumulating on the counters, ask yourself not only what kind of paper is gathering on the surfaces but also why it is landing there at all. Perhaps you don't have a workable home office, and paper is getting jammed up in the kitchen with nowhere else to go. If you see lots of bills and payment stubs among your piles, perhaps all your financial paperwork gets permanently stuck in the kitchen during and after the bill-paying process.

If you are dealing with the same issues in your home office and your kitchen, maybe the way you sort items is the problem. If you haven't taken the time yet to decide which kinds of paper you should sort in the office and which you should sort in the kitchen, paper will be more likely to travel throughout the house. To prevent wandering paper in our home, we've decided that only the initial mail sort should take place in the kitchen, but from there, all paper will proceed to the home office for processing.

Since being self-reflective and remembering to ask ourselves these ongoing questions is difficult as we are organizing, we often revert to our affinity for "cleaning up." We
square up the piles and stash clutter out of sight. Because we
tend to get off track without the necessary discovery process, some people decide to hire an expert to ensure that they
truly understand their organizing issues along the way. Our
clients who are the most successful at maintaining the systems they establish are the ones who take the time to understand their own habits. They have discovered how and why
they use their space the way they do.

Discovered Solutions vs. Imposed Solutions

Ever wonder why the "three steps to a perfect pantry"
article that you found in your favorite magazine let you
down? Frustrated that the card catalog system for organizing
chores that you read about in a book didn't work when you
tried it? You only have to try cookie-cutter, one-size-fits-all
organizing advice a few times before you realize that these
generalized solutions don't work.

Barbara is a client who needed organizing help in almost
every room of her home. As we were touring her space, we
found a half-finished, abandoned filing system flowing out of
her file cabinet. From the cabinet, the paper poured into
some wicker baskets and cardboard boxes and then onto the
floor. When I got down on my knees and began flipping
through her files, I realized that she had bought a do-it-yourself filing kit. It came with preprinted labels. The labels were
grouped into types and assigned a rainbow of colors. I
looked up at Barbara as we surveyed this project and she gri-
maced in frustration.

Barbara explained that she had bought all the supplies that the kit instructed her to purchase. Determined to tackle her mound of paper, she dove into the filing project with a vengeance. She wanted to make fast progress and charged ahead by sticking labels onto files. She had half the labels affixed before she started thinking about her paperwork, and she became confused.

The filing kit had separate labels for auto and home-owner's insurance, but her policy grouped them together, so she didn't know which of the two labels to use. The kit called her medical insurance "Healthcare," but that phrase didn't really make sense to Barbara. She hesitated to drop the medical insurance paperwork in the file for fear she would never find it again. Some of the labels didn't apply to her, and now she had nothing to put in those files that she had labeled. She had a growing stack of papers that didn't fit any of the preprinted labels, so she wasn't sure what to do with the orphaned files. This do-it-yourself filing kit seemed like a good idea at the time, but it wasn't a good fit for Barbara.

Cookie-cutter solutions that are supposed to apply universally never seem to work. A good discovery process will put the unique needs and thought process of the user at the center of the equation. When we impose other people's thought processes onto ourselves, we are unlikely to adapt to their thinking.

Even the individual features of a filing system should be person-specific. For example, color means different things to different people. Most people associate green with money, so they want their financial files to be green or at least have a green label. Others would insist that their financial files should be red because they want to stay out of the red!

Phrases and words are also extremely compelling, and different people are moved by different combinations of words. For example, I like brevity in labeling, so I might want to label my homeowners insurance simply "Homeowners," while my friend might think of the institution before she thinks of the type of insurance. She might want to label her homeowners insurance file "State Farm Insurance." Even the method of labeling should be tailored to the person using the filing system, based on whether they prefer paper, plastic, or handwritten labels. No approach to labeling is right or wrong because the solution should always be customized to the user.

In order for any organizing system to last, it absolutely must make intuitive sense to the user, or it will be abandoned. Imposed solutions don't work. Only solutions created through a discovery process will last.

An Organic Process

My team of organizers recently performed a space makeover on local television. We transformed an unsightly bonus room that was being used for haphazard storage into an attractive media room. All kinds of nomadic items landed in the basement bonus room, including remodeling remnants, memorabilia, and lots of superfluous stuff that was later donated. At the end of the bonus room was a storage closet, but we weren't sure initially how it would ultimately be used.

You might be surprised that from the beginning we didn't know how the closet would be used and what would go inside. After all, aren't we the specialists with all the answers? Yes and no. We have lots of ideas, strategies, and a methodology. Yet we know that each person and space has unique needs and challenges that we must organically discover. We are comfortable not having all the answers right away to an organizing challenge we may face. We know that by applying a good discovery process we will learn more as we get further into the project.

After we removed the remnants and junk, we moved in a couch, chaise, television, and end table. The big things that anchor a room were in place. The room began to take shape.

I originally thought that because the family didn't have a television stand in which to store electronic media, they could store the media in the storage closet. Once we sorted the contents of the room, however, we discovered that this family didn't actually have that many VHS tapes, DVDs, or music CDs after all. We realized dedicating a whole closet to only one box of tapes and disks wouldn't make sense.

We then speculated that the family could stow their memorabilia in the storage closet if the closet was big enough. On the other hand, the closet might be a perfect home for camera and video equipment or for games and puzzles. We weren't sure which option made the most sense, but we were confident that by progressing through the project organically we would find a solution for the electronic media and a sensible use for the storage closet.

We eventually decided that none of the above would live in the media room storage closet! We ended up storing household décor items and unused framed artwork in the closet. Why? As the project progressed, the couple decided to donate all their games and puzzles. They relocated the camera and video equipment to another room. Memorabilia found another home in an armoire.

The media room project demonstrates that good organizing is an organic process, one that develops as it progresses. This is great news for those who are disorganized and who fear the process. You don't have to know all the answers before you begin organizing! Rather than a goal or a list of tasks, organizing is actually a natural, organic process in which you explore what works for you and what doesn't.

If you have been putting off your organizing journey because you felt you had to be an expert with all the answers, you can let yourself off the hook. If you have ever felt that organizing is an insurmountable list of goals to achieve, toss out the list. I invite you to embrace organizing as an organic process that allows you to fail. In failing, you will discover what does *not* work and, by process of elimination, what *does* work for you!

Self-Awareness Process

What's Really Going On Here?

Lest you think that all my clients have straightforward organizing challenges that are easily resolved with a little discovery, organic progression, and elbow grease, read on! Ann's small condo is packed to the rafters with stuff. From books and CDs, to home décor, to her teacup collection, Ann has accumulated more items than many stores have in inventory.

In order to meet with Ann, I have to carve a path through her entry hall, step over the dog, and sit gingerly on the very edge of a sofa (or is it a loveseat?). The seat is filled with mounds of paper and 14 pillows. I notice that since my last visit, she has collected more candles. She owns more candles than one person could burn in a lifetime. Ann's accumulation is amazingly prolific.

At every visit, Ann complains that she isn't making much progress on her organizing projects and seems frustrated that I haven't shared the secret silver bullet of organizing bliss. I softly remind Ann that all our previous progress has been blanketed by a new layer of accumulation. She shakes her head and reasons that the systems we set up weren't really working anyway. She acknowledges that she has been shopping, but she points to several plastic bags in the hall and insists that she plans on returning some of her purchases. She has good intentions but lacks follow-through. More to the point, Ann has a serious shopping problem. (Ann also struggles with a condition known as Chronic Disorganization, which we discussed in chapter 3, "The Disorder Disease." If Ann's struggles seem too close to home, visit the National Study Group on Chronic Disorganization website at www.nsgcd.org.)

Even with systems in place to help her manage her growing mess, Ann cannot make any lasting progress until she addresses her shopping addiction. When Ann feels depressed, she hops in the car and goes to the store. When she feels trapped in the ever-increasing mounds, she escapes to the mall. But fleeing her home doesn't seem to help. For organizing success, Ann must recognize and change her behavior.

Know Thyself

The term "self-awareness" has taken on a New Age, transcendental meaning these days. I'm not recommending this approach, which can quickly leave you adrift on a sea of relativism. I'm talking about a good old-fashioned reality check. I'm talking about being brave enough to look in the mirror. If you really want to know why you can't get organized, you can usually find the answers by enlisting a friend, a family member, or an objective outsider to help you discover the truth.

What have you tried before to get organized? Why do you think it didn't work? Did you set up systems that made sense to you, or did you try cookie-cutter, one-size-fits-all solutions? Did you practice the discipline of maintenance? What habits are you holding onto that may be standing in your way of achieving an orderly life? Until you get serious about leaving your baggage at the curb, you will likely drag your self-defeating habits into a disorganized future.

Self-observation is one key to setting up and maintaining systems. Good organizing is always the result of good self-observation. The further you venture into your organizing process, the more you will learn about yourself.

Your environment usually reflects the tapestry of your life. If your time and schedule are out of control, your home and office will likely be littered with unprocessed paper and other items you haven't put away. If you've recently endured the passing of a loved one, your home may be clogged with inherited belongings. If you're living in the past, the vestiges of days gone by may be lurking in your home, holding you back from moving forward. Your stuff and calendar are mirrors of what is going on inside your life.

Play Defense

Self-awareness includes understanding the factors that have caused disorder in your life. It also includes knowing and working with your own unique habits and patterns. We can learn to anticipate our own behavior and move defensively against our propensity for disorder.

Observe where you tend to fail, and remove the possibility of feeling like a failure. Instead of berating yourself for always piling your shoes in the doorway, work with your natural habit, and place a basket there to capture the shoes. Reward yourself while you are performing maintenance tasks. Rather than resisting a chore by saying, "I have no time to unload the dishwasher," take those three minutes to heat microwave popcorn and unload the dishes while you wait for your snack. When you notice that the kids' toys are beginning to creep all over the house again, choose to be proactive instead of giving up. Institute a weekly roundup in which you can enlist your children in a fun activity that teaches them organizing and maintenance skills. Responding to your natural habits and living patterns will help you defend against disorder.

If you want to create order out of your chaotic environment, start by changing your thinking and begin working *with* yourself instead of against yourself. As the natural world demonstrates, things naturally move from order to chaos, so we must play defense if we want to stay ahead in the game. When you recognize your habits and patterns and begin to work with them, you can have daily victory. Don't give up—the reward for embracing organizing as a process is your own liberation!

8

The Pain Principle

If you are opening this chapter with trepidation, wondering why an organizing book has a chapter on pain, let me put your mind at ease. This chapter is not about misery, nor do I want you to associate organizing your life with ongoing pain. However, as I've begun figuring out why people don't get organized, I've realized that the answer has a lot to do with pain avoidance. Therefore, to reclaim your life you need to consider the possibility of some pain.

Of course, you might love to organize. You might think organizing is fun and rewarding, and in that case, you might not need this chapter. However, learning some concepts I share in this chapter might be helpful, such as the Pain Tunnel and the fact that things get worse before they get better when you're organizing. The Pain Principle will also help you help your children, coworkers, or loved ones overcome their own disorganization.

Organizing brings the rest of us varying degrees of pain. Some people find organizing annoying and a little painful, so they attempt to organize their space and belongings only when the situation has become critical. Even the efforts they do make don't last because they don't address how they got in the mess they're in. They slap together solutions that tide them over, but don't address the real problems. They also struggle with maintenance because they don't really see the connection between protecting their systems and their quality of life. They are likely to pay the price with a messy space and a cluttered mind.

Others find organizing their space and life acutely painful, and though their life is closing in on them, they are paralyzed from even thinking about organizing. These folks use many tactics to resist making time for organizing, including avoidance and rebellion. For them, dealing with the chaotic status quo is less painful than facing and tackling their disorganization.

The Pain Principle is this: If you can understand why and how pain works to keep you from organizing your life, then you can address it head-on and create a plan for overcoming it. Those of us who are avoiding organizing because it is painful will never make lasting changes in our environment or life. We will continue to peck away at the problem, only to find ourselves stuck in the same self-defeating cycle of disorder. Only when we understand why we are resisting organizing and resolve to embrace the process can we create and maintain organized systems.

Why Can Organizing Be Painful?

Organizing can be painful because it can cause fear, it makes us slow down, and it requires commitment. Of course, some people are organizing junkies, and no mess or pile is insurmountable. Their minds see solutions when they encounter an organizing challenge. These are the people I look for as employees of my organizing company!

However, you may never have learned organizing skills and struggle to find answers to your organizing problems. You've purchased products and have thrown them at the problem. You've spent many weekends tidying up, and the mess just comes right back. You hate to spend your precious free time organizing when you are good at and enjoy doing so many other things. Organizing makes you feel frustrated and overwhelmed, so you push it to the bottom of your to-do list.

Why are some activities so easy to engage in while others are painful? We engage in the activities we like and that offer a payoff. We choose activities we don't have to discipline ourselves to accomplish. The need to consistently organize our environment and our life continually presses our pain button, and we react accordingly. Family members wait for one another to unload the dishwasher or fold the laundry because these are grindingly ongoing, low-payoff tasks. Clothes from two decades ago sit in our closets because we are delaying the pain of admitting we are never going to get back to that size. Our garages are packed with the vestiges of our past, our excess, other people's stuff, and our good intentions. We don't take the time to clear them out—because that would be painful.

As I've explored the question of why people don't get organized, I've found that most people are adverse to dedicating time and energy to something that causes them angst and that's perfectly natural. If they have to slow down and be purposeful about an activity, they often avoid it. They also instinctively know that an organizing project will require their attention and energy, so they resist even starting. This too is natural. However, if you don't examine *why* you're not addressing the problems that are compromising your lifestyle, you are unlikely to reclaim your quality of life.

We're Afraid

We may not identify the reason we're resisting organizing as fear, but when we get right down to it, we're afraid. We are afraid to start our organizing projects because they are overwhelming to us. With so much to do, the scope of the project seems beyond our capabilities. We are stuck in our tracks because we don't know where to begin. We've let things pile up so long that we don't know how we can possibly dig out. We know that we will have to face every single thing we've set aside. The thought of having to pay the piper is overpowering, so we stay in our pain. However uncomfortable the chaos is, we reason that it can't be as bad as exposing it and dealing with it.

There is something spiritual about the way we behave toward our organization. Think about it: When we do things in our personal life we aren't proud of, we keep secrets about them. We keep our skeletons in dark closets. Until we bring those things to light and deal with them, however, we are in a prison of fear and self-condemnation. We cannot receive forgiveness from God, ourselves, and others until we confess and deal with the consequences. However bad the fallout may be in dealing with our mistakes, the secrets that trap us are far worse.

I've found that people act the same way about their disorganization if it has gone beyond their control. At home, we keep secrets about it and stop inviting people over. At work, we make excuses about it and hunker down in defeat. We are ashamed of our mess. We live in fear and self-condemnation about our disorganization, and we refuse to face it head-on because of that fear. If we are avoiding or rebelling against organizing, then deep down we probably fear the process. Until we expose our organizing issues, we can't experience liberation from our prison of disorder.

When we don't know how to do something, we avoid it so we don't have to feel incompetent. I don't join in poker games with my husband's friends because I never learned how to play poker, and I don't want to look stupid or be forced to ask a hundred questions. I don't want to snowboard because I feel confident on skis, and I don't want to start over learning something from scratch. Similarly, when we behold a big pile of paper that we have amassed and we don't know how to tackle it, we simply avoid it.

Other people suffer from perfectionism. If we can't get our systems perfect, why even try? You might be surprised to learn that some of the messiest homes I've seen are inhabited by perfectionists! The perfectionist who has hired me to organize her home is actually tortured by her chaos because she envisions a flawless space, and she can't live up to her own ideals. She doesn't just want an accessible, organized closet; she wants a built-in, color-coded, labeled, and beautifully decorated closet. Because she can't afford a built-in system and all the lovely accessories, she figures organizing the closet is a waste of her time. Instead of beginning an imperfect, organic process as we discussed in the last chapter, the perfectionist waits to begin a perfect process with a guaranteed outcome. Of course, this process doesn't exist.

Whether we know it or not, we may be victims of fear. Have you been putting off your organizing projects because

you are overwhelmed, you lack the skills, or you are a perfectionist? If so, you will stay stuck in your prison of disorganization until you resolve to break out!

One way to overcome fear is to think rationally about it.
What is the worst thing that could happen? Perhaps you
might fail. So what's so irreparable about that? You can
always start again. Perhaps you might confirm that you don't
have the skills. You can always bring in an expert. On the
other hand, what is the worst thing that could happen if you
did nothing? We all know the answer to this one: You will
stay behind the bars of your disorganization indefinitely. So
which is worse, trying and failing (with the likelihood of success) or not trying at all?

We Expect Ease and Speed

We hate waiting in line because we want to be served
now. We despise traffic jams because we don't want to face
obstacles in our mission to get somewhere. We are a culture
that hates to wait, hates to have our time wasted, and hates to
put off reward. We want what we want, and we want it now.

We are used to receiving enticingly easy solutions to our
problems. We can get virtually anything we want whenever
we want it. Many restaurants, services, and even fitness centers are now open 24 hours a day. Instead of calling someone
with a question, we can usually look it up online and get an
immediate answer. Thanks to pagers, cell phones, and wire-
less devices, we can communicate remotely. With a culture
that values total access and emphasizes speed, we can easily
perceive that we deserve to have our own needs and desires
met immediately at all times. Don't get me wrong—I love
modern conveniences, but like many of us, I have begun to
turn conveniences into expectations.

Organizing can be painful to some of us simply because it is foreign to our daily pace and stretches our comfort zone. Most of us are used to a fast-paced life, and we see the results of our work fairly quickly. We zip off e-mails and voice mails by the dozens and often get instant responses. We are super-charged for activity and have short attention spans. True organizing requires us to slow down, reflect on the causes of our disorganization, and set up thoughtful systems built around our lifestyle.

Our frenetic pace and our demand for ease can make organizing seem like a chore. We hate chores but love rewards. The quick tips for organizing offered in the market-place placate our human desire for a speedy fix. Wired for speed, we like the idea—however unrealistic it may be—that organizing can be done in a few simple steps.

If you've been conditioned by ease and speed but want to reclaim your life, consider that organizing is an investment in your quality of life, not a chore. Think about the things that matter most in life. They require an investment of time and energy, but they are well worth the effort. Fulfilling relationships develop with time and attention. Beautiful architecture is not built overnight. Lush gardens require planting and tending and watering. When you make an investment, you will reap the dividends!

We're Not Ready to Commit

In addition to requiring an investment, organizing requires commitment. We have to allocate time, decisions, and maintenance to the process if we want to find success. Since we might think organizing is scary, unpleasant, or slow, we avoid it so that we can spend time on things we enjoy.

We'd gladly take a quick tip, but we don't want to commit to a process. Committing to organizing seems like a sentence to some of us who are commitment adverse.

Organizing is time-consuming, and we know it! We can tell that an hour or two is not going to make a dent, and we overestimate how long the project will actually take. Most projects take between six and twenty hours. A kitchen pantry or hall closet might only take two or three hours, but we might spend 24 hours digging out and setting up good systems in a deeply buried home office. Yet we estimate that an organizing project will take a month of Sundays. Telling ourselves that our project will take more time than it actually will allows us to use the excuse that we just don't have the time to set aside. This is one way we deal with the fear of an overwhelming project: We knowingly or unknowingly overestimate how long it will take in order to avoid it.

My neighbors told me that they resist organizing their garage because that would require them to make too many decisions. They've put off corralling their clutter because they need to toss some of the junk and donate some of it. They need to relocate some of their garage stuff within the home. Rather than lining up their belongings and making decisions, they let the mess pile up because that's easier. However, they hate the way the clutter looks, and it causes static in their marriage! They are paying the price every day for not being willing to make decisions.

Like my neighbors, we all do self-defeating things just to avoid making decisions. Why do we put off decisions? Are we afraid we will make the wrong decision? Do decisions require too much of our time? Do we honestly not know the answers? We must figure out why we are procrastinating on making decisions if we want to break out of this cycle of buildup. Think about it: You will eventually need to deal with every item that you set aside and every paper that you shuffle in order for you to overcome the clutter. So quit delaying those decisions, and you will save yourself a lot of digging out later on!

Recently I spoke with a prospective client on the phone. When I explained that we partner with our clients to create change, she was annoyed that our staff wouldn't just come to her office and organize it for her. She wanted us to tackle her organizing problems without her. A fast-paced business owner, she felt she didn't have time to invest setting up her systems. I could hardly keep her attention as she fretted about my quote of 12 to 20 hours to organize her office. She agonized over the thought of taking away that much time from her clients to invest in the process of establishing orderly systems.

Finally, I told her straightforwardly that only those who are committed to restoring their quality of life can get and stay organized. Something clicked for her when I said that, and she began sharing how badly she feels that she hasn't kept up with her past clients. She admitted that though her business was extremely profitable, she had no personal life at all. In that call, she crossed over the commitment barrier with her own desire to reclaim her life. She saw that organizing her business would actually alleviate the daily pain she experiences. If you want to restore your quality of life, a commitment to organizing will be the first step.

Pain Tunnel

The reason most of us don't embrace the true process of organizing is that deep down we know it really isn't going to be a quick fix, but we are hoping we can circumvent the hard work. We associate the hard work of organizing with pain. We want to go around it, above it, beside it, or below it, but *please,* not through it. Our natural proclivity is to avoid pain. Authentic organizing, however, can be (and perhaps even should be) painful.

When I was little, my brother and I used to ride our bikes around town. We would weave through parks and neighborhoods and shoot through pedestrian tunnels. We used to hold our breath as we zipped through the rippled metal tubes that formed the tunnels. Sometimes the tubes were just a few feet long, and sometimes they were so long they were dark inside. The short tunnels were fine by me, but the long ones really freaked me out. Fortunately, my brother would take the lead, and I would just have to pedal furiously to keep up.

The short tunnel represents the organizing process for those who enjoy organizing or only have a small backlog of disorganization. They shoot through their process fairly rapidly and get to the other side with little angst. The long tunnel represents the organizing process for those who loathe the exposure and decisions and commitment true organizing requires.

The organizing process is the Pain Tunnel for those who have been resisting establishing systems and ordering their lives. They don't want to examine their causes of disorder, make scores of decisions, and invest for the long haul. Figuratively speaking, they would rather leap over the tunnel, dodge the tunnel, or even dig a channel under the tunnel. They want to do anything to avoid pain, like buying tons of products to fix the problem, applying a few quick tips, or paying someone else to do it for them.

In order to get all the way through the Pain Tunnel, you cannot venture inside and then back out. Many people have hired us to tackle their disorganization, but after a few appointments their fears or life demands cause them to back out of the Pain Tunnel. We are disappointed when we have taken clients by the hand, pointed out the light at the end of the tunnel, promised to guide them through, started out on our journey...and then they retreat. People have their own reasons for retreating, and we don't judge them. We regret their decision for their sake because we know they can't emerge from their struggle until they cross over the opposing side of their tunnel.

True and lasting order doesn't come without the struggle against self that leads to change. Without learning about ourselves, becoming aware of our habits, and facing the costs of our disorganization, we cannot emerge from our state of disorder. As we struggle through our process, we gain skills and make new commitments to establish and protect our quality of life. Once we have gone through the pain, we don't particularly want to repeat it, so we become more committed to maintenance.

If you are debating about entering into your own Pain Tunnel of organization, or if you're partway in and considering backing out, I encourage you to continue! Bravely face whatever is inside the tunnel in order to overcome it. Inside the tunnel is where you will deal with the backlog—all the stuff that has been piling up. Inside the tunnel you will face fear, decisions, and commitment issues. You will be challenged to figure out what works for you and to create it. You will pick up organizational skills you never learned from parents or teachers. When you emerge, you will be more equipped for dealing with information and tasks than ever before. You will be able to identify and live by your priorities. A reclaimed life will be your reward for going through the Pain Tunnel.

It Gets Worse Before It Gets Better

People sometimes don't like finding out that the organizing process can actually cause chaos for a while. When our professional organizers begin working with clients, we try to set their expectations properly. We want to make sure they know how the organizing process may affect their household or their business. We want them to know that their space might look worse temporarily before it gets better.

For example, when we organize a kitchen, we have to remove everything from the space, which means that we will need a staging area. As we remove items from the cabinets, we are storing them by type in boxes or baskets. Everything from nonperishable food to dishes to appliances will cover their kitchen floor for a short time while we are sorting and tossing. We may even need floor space in an adjoining room to stage some of our boxes. We will then wipe down all the cabinets and purchase the appropriate storage containers and tools to maximize space.

During the process, the kitchen may appear as if a small bomb has gone off! Access to items might be limited for a short time and the client might have to eat out for a night. Some clients are overwhelmed when they pull everything out from behind closed doors and see it covering their space. For this reason, we try to book back-to-back appointments for large projects like kitchens and garages. We don't want the client's interim pain to last too long! By preparing people for the fact that things can get worse before they get better, we help them take the temporary mess in stride while they keep the end goal in sight.

If you fear that your mess might become worse if you begin to get organized, you may be perfectly right! However, it will only get worse for a very short time. Once you've reached the crest, everything else is downhill. Once the sorting, grouping, and eliminating is finished, the plan comes together.

Pain Relief Strategies

Now that we understand why organizing is painful, let's look at some strategies to get through the pain. As you know from the Pain Tunnel model, you cannot overcome your disorganization and achieve lasting success until you experience the process. However, you may not know where to begin.

Plan

Recently I met with Tom, who was totally overwhelmed at home and at work. I guesstimated that we would spend several months establishing workable systems in both locations because he could only work with us once or twice a month. I could tell that Tom was defeated by the thought of taking so long to restore order.

To give him hope, I recommended to Tom that we summarize the scope of his home and office projects first. Then I advised that we make a list of short-term action steps for each environment. We established a "relief plan" for his home and another for his office. His relief plans contained the action steps we would take toward the goal of organizing his entire household and professional office space. To Tom, the scope of the projects seemed insurmountable, but the short-term action steps gave him something to focus on for now.

A scope-of-project assessment includes all the various rooms, challenges, or projects we will tackle. Remember, organizing is an organic process, so some of these projects may later drop off your list, and new ones may emerge. Keeping sight of the scope of your project is important so that you don't lose sight of your goals. By keeping an eye on the big picture, you can strategically, progressively tackle all your organizing projects. Without an understanding of the scope of your project, on the other hand, you might enter the Pain Tunnel only to back right out again because you feel overwhelmed.

A multiplicity of projects can be overwhelming to someone who is averse to the pain of organizing, so I recommend devising short-term action steps to achieve one project at a time. Relief plans can keep the momentum going when you face a monumental task. Relief plans offer achievable steps.

Relief plans can also be valuable if you face an event that is sure to cause chaos in your life. When loved ones die and you have to clear out their home and deal with a whole new set of decisions, you need a relief plan. When you are in transition between jobs and are managing a job search, you need a relief plan. When you are going through a remodel and are dealing with a flood of remodeling paperwork and the imposition on your household, you need a relief plan. Your chances of successfully navigating a chaotic life event and protecting the systems you've worked so hard to establish are significantly higher with a relief plan.

Partner

We've all found that difficult times are often easier to weather with another person by your side cheering you on. If you are committed to getting organized, you will benefit from accountability and support. Whether you partner with a friend or an expert you will find comfort and guidance for your organizing process. The simple presence of another person encourages us to stay focused and press on.

Partner with a Friend

As I will discuss in chapter 13: "Take an Aerial View," we were built for community. We group together for camaraderie and protection. Sticking together feels safer than going it alone. For this reason, choosing a friend with whom you can undertake your organizing adventure makes sense.

When choosing your organizing friend, look for someone who demonstrates compassion and encouragement. You don't want to feel embarrassed or beat down about lack of progress; you want someone who won't judge you and who will inspire you to do better. Try to find someone who struggles with similar issues, like paper piling, or has a similar scope of project. If you have a whole-house project and you partner with someone who needs only to organize a tiny closet, the rapid completion of his or her project might make you feel defeated.

Partner with an Expert

Sometimes your organizing needs may exceed a friend's expertise. Don't be afraid to seek the help of a professional when necessary. You may need therapy from a counselor for a shopping addiction. You may need design services like an architectural rendering from an interior designer. You may need help from a professional organizer to build paper and information management systems. If you simply need skills that your friend can't offer, bring in an expert to consult with you. To find an organizer, see page 254.

You have officially completed The Pain Principle, and it wasn't so bad, was it? I hope you are now equipped with a better understanding of why you may have resisted getting organized. By addressing your resistance head-on, you can allow reason to triumph and embrace organizing as a liberating process.

9

The Preparation Principle

Janet is a busy mom of four teenage boys. Her household feels like a zoo most of the time. She spends her days picking pop cans and empty snack cartons off the coffee tables, returning videos to the store, plucking dirty clothes off the floor, doing laundry, running errands, and grocery shopping. She constantly cleans up after her children at home. She has become a 24-hour concierge service for her children.

Meetings and appointments often never make it onto Janet's calendar. She and her husband have season tickets to the ballet, but they frequently miss these expensive events because they lost the tickets or didn't write down the event dates. The ballet schedule is in a pile somewhere along with overdue bills, lost tickets, and important correspondence. In fact, she has many piles of paper throughout the house. Janet is buried with paper, and she never manages to get through all the mail. No wonder she can never process it all—she is constantly interrupted by a family member needing immediate assistance.

Janet dreams of starting an interior decorating business, but she just can't seem to find the time. Between running errands and running the household, her family absorbs her time. She loves decorating her own home and wonders if she has what it takes to decorate for others. Whenever these thoughts enter her mind, she savors them for a while but then pushes them to the back burner as she deals with the next adolescent emergency.

Recently, Janet's family was supposed to go on vacation to Florida. As usual, the family was behind schedule, and no one had packed in advance. The day of their trip, the boys slept in, and Janet was distracted with cleaning up after the boys. As the day wore on, Janet casually started looking for their plane tickets. Upon finding the tickets under a pile of mail, her heart started racing when she read the departure time. The flight left in an hour, and they lived 45 minutes from the airport! Frantically, she ran around the house yelling at the boys to get out of bed. No one had time to pack even one bag! They grouchily piled into the car with only the clothes on their backs.

"Why did you even consider going without your stuff?" I asked in amazement when Janet shared this story with me. Janet replied that they figured they would buy clothes when they arrived in Florida. "What about your cosmetics and toothbrush, and all that stuff?" I persisted. "Oh, we just had to find a pharmacy when we got there, and we bought that stuff too," Janet told me. "It wasn't that big of a deal." I inferred from her nonchalance that their lack of preparation and the ensuing consequences were an accepted way of life in her household.

If Janet's situation sounds familiar, our next organizing principle may inspire you to change your habits. If you find yourself living haphazardly, you can put an end to wasteful ways and reclaim your boundaries. Through preparation, you can get ready for action and become available to live your dreams. The Preparation Principle is this: Choosing organization for your life can help you reclaim control and equip you for opportunity.

Reclaim Control

End the Wastefulness

Like many of us, Janet rarely stops to count the cost of her disorganized and slapdash lifestyle. Her family's lack of preparedness causes numerous financial consequences. When they purchased belongings they already owned because they didn't pack for their trip, they incurred costs. Late fees on lost, unpaid bills continually damage their credit rating. Janet forgets to write down the boys' appointment dates with doctors, dentists, and counselors, so she must often pay fees for missing the appointments. Though Janet feels guilty about these charges, she reasons that she "just couldn't get to it" and goes on with her day. Janet even wastes her gas as urgent demands incessantly interrupt her driving route. All of these unconscious choices add up to wasteful living.

Living in a disorganized, reactive manner causes us to make poor choices with our time and money. Like Janet, we experience the bleeding of waste. When we live without thinking about the consequences, we usually incur a cost. We often dismiss the sensitive subject of how our choices affect our finances. Janet's family doesn't learn from the financial consequences of their haphazard lifestyle, so the consequences keep coming.

Wastefulness Survey

Below is an exercise that will provide an informal reality check regarding your own wastefulness. Sit down with a pen, paper, and calculator and add up the waste in your life on a monthly basis. Don't get stuck on coming up with exact numbers; this is meant to provide a guesstimate of wasted resources.

Late fees on bills _____

Definition: The charges you are assessed for not remitting payment on time.

Examples: You were late on sending in the mortgage and your lender assessed a $60 penalty. You had to pay a fee to your phone company to reactivate your service after they turned it off.

Missed appointment fees _____

Definition: The charges you are assessed for missing appointments or canceling them too late.

Examples: You forgot to record the appointment with the counselor on your calendar, missed the appointment, and had to pay for the full appointment even though you received no service.

Wasted gas money _____ *miles wasted @ $.* ____/ *mile =* _____ *total expense* (To compensate for gas and wear and tear on your vehicle, we recommend multiplying your miles by the current IRS mileage reimbursement formula.)

Definition: Miles you incurred going out of your way or with inefficient routes or for unexpected reasons due to lack of planning.

Examples: You get halfway to your destination and have to turn around because you've forgotten something at work or at home, and now you have to travel twice as far. You are across town and have to run an unexpected errand for your kid that takes an additional 20 miles each way.

Wasted utilities _____

Definition: Charges from your various utility providers, like phone, water, sewer, electricity, natural gas, and water that were unnecessary.

Examples: You accidentally left the heat on while you were gone on vacation. You have an outrageous cell phone plan, and you've never called your service provider to ask for a better deal or shopped around for lower rates.

Replacement costs _____

Definition: Purchasing goods that you already own to replace goods that you've lost or left behind.

Examples: When you can't find the sleeping bag that you know you own, you buy a new one. When traveling, you forget to pack items that you already own and have to purchase duplicates. You purchase a gift for someone, stash it somewhere, forget about it, and then have to repurchase the gift.

Overbuying _____

Definition: Purchasing too much of something. Warehouse stores encourage buying overages.

Examples: You don't stop for a few minutes to make a grocery list before you shop, and you come home with perishable items that you don't use in time and that spoil as a result. You purchase more toys than your children can use or enjoy, and the toys are outgrown or cast aside.

The cost of your time _____ *wasted hours @ $* _____ *your hourly rate = total expense* (This is a tough one for a lot of people because we often think our time is free. However, if you are [or were to be] gainfully employed, insert your approximate hourly rate above and multiply by your average wasted hours per month [hint: most people waste at least an hour per day].)

Definition: Time spent wastefully.

Examples: You spend an hour looking for your keys, a file folder, or a kid's lost glove. You left something behind and have to spend an additional half hour of your time retrieving that item. You have to re-create an electronic document you lost.

At the very least, this little survey can give you an idea of the areas of waste that you may be experiencing. After you've totaled up your wasted dollars in a month, you can multiply that figure by 12 to determine how much you may be wasting per year. You may be shocked by how much money slips away through waste.

Because we are ill-prepared and disorganized, we unknowingly flush money down the toilet every month. Seeing how much money we waste might be painful, but we often have to reach a point of pain before we change our habits. The good news is that by becoming aware of the waste, you can take action to eliminate the nagging fear and anxiety many of us suffer from when we are disorganized. You are in the process of reclaiming your life! You can get smart and put an end to the wastefulness in your life!

Establish Boundaries

Now that Janet's sons have their driver's licenses, they frequently rent videos from the video store. After watching the videos, the boys move on to other entertainment, and the tapes or DVDs remain in the machine. The boys don't return the videos to the store or even rewind them! They don't realize returning the videos is their job; they expect that Mom will take care of it.

At last count, their fees for late videos was in the hundreds of dollars! Janet is annoyed and anxious that they have incurred these fees, so she rants and raves at the boys. But in the end, she is the one who rewinds and repackages the videos and takes them back to the store. The late fees are charged to the family's account, which comes out of Janet's pocket. The boys rarely feel the consequences of their actions, so the same scene is replayed over and over in their household.

Janet's boys take advantage of her and her time because she allows them to. She doesn't insist that her sons take responsibility for their own actions. Their bad behavior brings no consequences, at least for them. Janet, however, is unknowingly paying their consequences as she races to the store to return the videos and as she pays the bill for their late fees.

If other people's actions are contributing to your disorganization, you may need to establish some better boundaries for yourself. I'm no counselor or therapist, so I can't tell you what kind of boundaries you need to establish in your home or work environment. You probably already know what needs to happen, but for a variety of reasons, you've been living with the status quo. If others are helping cause your chaos, you've either got to continue living with it or make a change. We all know we can't change others, so you'll have to change yourself if you want to reclaim your disorganized life. Only you can set and honor your own boundaries.

Is lack of boundaries a common trait among the disorganized? I'm not a psychologist, nor have I done any scientific research, but my guess is yes. Over and over again, our professional organizers meet disorganized people who tell us through their stories that they lack personal boundaries. Lack of boundaries causes reactive living, prevents proper preparation, and creates all kinds of chaos. Organization is not about having a neat and tidy environment; it's about taking responsibility for yourself and managing your choices each day so you can live by your priorities.

Equip Yourself for Opportunity

My husband, Trevor, is an electrician, skilled in residential, commercial, and industrial work. His employer appreciates that Trevor is a fast and efficient worker who will get jobs done quickly so the business can make money. Jobs with a tight budget require hard workers who come prepared. Trevor often goes out on service calls to residential customers. He zips around town in the company van helping troubleshoot electrical problems, installing light fixtures, adding outlets, and upgrading service. His van is packed to the gills with tools and material. It is a shop on wheels!

Prepare for Action

When Trevor shows up to a job, he often doesn't know what supplies he will need until he sees the scope of the project. If he has planned ahead and stocked his van with supplies, he is more likely to have the resources he needs to complete the job. If he is lacking even a few small pieces, he must leave the job and go to the local electrical supply store to replenish his stock and return to the job site. Most jobs are priced with time and materials, so the homeowner pays extra if Trevor doesn't have the materials needed for the job. However, if the job was bid with a flat fee as a two-hour project and his trip to the store took an additional hour, his company loses money on the job. Either way, lack of preparation costs someone, and neither the homeowner nor the company wants to waste money.

In addition to having all the appropriate tools and materials, Trevor also needs to keep his van organized so he can find everything he needs and get the job done fast. When his van is a mess, he has to dig for the equipment and parts the project requires. Pawing through layers of material not only produces a bigger mess but also makes the job take twice as long. The longer the job takes, the more the homeowner pays or the company loses. In order to be ready for anything, Trevor tries to keep his van organized for action!

Preparation is as necessary in the professional workplace as it is in the trades. We all know that prepared professionals who plan ahead tend to do better in presentations and win more big accounts than those who are not prepared. Organized and efficient professionals earn raises and praises as their credibility increases and their colleagues vest more trust in them. On the other hand, workers who are poorly prepared tend to lose out on professional opportunities and earn more criticism than praise. The organized and prepared employee maximizes each project and earns more opportunities for work in the future.

Make Yourself Available

Remember Janet's secret ambition to become an interior decorator? She has plenty of financial resources to take classes, and her social connections could form an instant client base. However, Janet isn't pursuing her professional dreams because her attention is entirely absorbed by other people's demands. She spends her time catering to her nearly grown children and trying to get a handle on her out-of-control household. Janet has the time to follow her dreams, but she isn't *making room in her life* for her dreams.

When we encounter an outstanding opportunity, we usually drop everything to accommodate the prospect. When we're asked to do something we've always wanted to do, we find the time. Living in an orderly way creates space in our schedule and our life. Preparation equips us to recognize and seize opportunities that come along. When we create availability in our lives, we can pursue our dreams.

From time to time, we've all felt overloaded and experienced bunker mentality. In the bunker, people are interested in self-protection and survival. In wartime, the bunker is a necessary place of retreat and safety. Sadly, however, many of us operate in bunker mentality in our homes and businesses even when we don't need to. We shut ourselves into our daily routines and operate in survival mode.

Janet is living in a bunker of her own making. She is too disorganized and distracted by others to look up and see the possibilities in her life. If Janet decided that launching her own design business was a priority for her, she could reclaim her time for her own use. She would need to slow down her harried pace and purposely invest some time to prepare the infrastructure for her business. She would need to help her children take responsibility for themselves by allowing them to take the consequences for their own actions. Once she reclaimed her time, she could become available to prepare for and pursue her decorating career.

Prepared or Defeated

Preparation is one facet of living in order. When you are prepared, you are attentive and ready for action. You are honoring your boundaries and making yourself available when you are prepared. Preparation helps you avoid living wastefully and squandering your time and resources. When you plan ahead and take proactive initiative, you are prepared to live life to its fullest. If you want to reclaim your personal or professional life, you can apply the Preparation Principle to improve your quality of life.

Not surprisingly, a spiritual connection exists between preparation and orderly living. When we are living in chaos and confusion, we are unfulfilled and ineffective. The distraction of our disorder robs our joy for life. We don't develop our spiritual life because we are constantly preoccupied with our physical and emotional life.

If you are living a frenzied and distracted life, you may have little room for a relationship with God. If you've been longing for a deeper spiritual life, you can begin the process now! You can redirect your life and set it on a new course. By investing some time to set up orderly systems to manage your life, you will create the physical and mental space to discover and enjoy your life priorities. Once you have more room in your life to pursue the things that truly matter, you can nurture your spiritual life as well.

Our time is limited, and the way we use it is meaningful. In the Bible, the apostle Paul encourages his friends, "Be very careful, then, how you live—not as unwise but as wise, making the most of every opportunity, because the days are evil" (Ephesians 5:15-16). Wise people use their time to prepare their lives for the things that truly matter.

10

The Pruning Principle

I think Trevor murdered our hydrangeas last year. That man is like a chainsaw killer when he starts pruning. He gets on a roll, and pretty soon piles of branches and foliage are separated forever from their life source. He gathers up the piles and hauls them off to the recycler, proud of the decimation he has left behind. Why is it that cutting out the old stuff makes us feel so good? What is so therapeutic about thinning stuff out?

Something about eliminating useless stuff just feels right. When we disentangle dead branches from a growing tree, we pull out the matter that is no longer good. When we cut back the yellowed reeds of a perennial flower, we know that its energy returns to its bulb. Ridding plants of the superfluous material makes us feel good about restoring them to health.

This kind of trimming feels good for a reason. Cutting out that which isn't useful in our life is a spiritual experience! The Bible applies the metaphor of pruning to our spiritual life. Jesus explains: "I am the true vine, and my Father is the gardener. He cuts off every branch in me that bears no fruit, while every branch that does bear fruit he prunes so that it will be even more fruitful" (John 15:1-2). Here we see that the gardener's purpose for cutting out deadwood and pruning back living stock is to produce more life and fruit. We shouldn't be surprised that spiritual principles prove true in our experience of the physical world as well.

The Pruning Principle is this: We will flourish in our personal, spiritual, and physical life when we expose ourselves and our environment to frequent pruning. Organizing, then, is not simply sorting, categorizing, and tossing, as many believe. Authentic organizing includes a purposeful and ongoing process of elimination and refinement.

Cut Out the Deadwood

We all have excess stuff in our life. You know what I'm talking about. We have too much junk stuffed into our homes. Paper that we haven't looked at in years fills our offices. Even our calendar is chock full of deadwood—stuff that simply drains our lives of energy. It clogs up our mental and emotional world. It blocks us from being productive. In order for us to get organized, we have to prune the deadwood in our lives.

Get Realistic About Your Stuff

Art teachers have a special organizing affliction—or is it an addiction? Our beloved instructors of art usually suffer from a supersized pack rat disease. Of course, art teachers are also imaginative, resourceful, and inventive, and obviously not all art teachers are pack rats. They transfer their array of creative skills to enrich our lives.

However, many art instructors are savers extraordinaire, and they accumulate as many supplies as they can and keep them as long as they can. The rest of the population sees empty jars of baby food to recycle, but the art teacher sees a mini soil-potting project. We see old clothespins, but the art teacher pictures the miniature Christmas reindeer her students could make. The rest of us would toss broken vacuum pieces, but the art teacher is fascinated by their forms and dreams up a lesson on shapes. Art educators accumulate piles of old magazines because they are excellent sources for collages. Even old clothes and linens are not safe from the art teacher's reach because they could be torn up and used as rags, painted on, or used as smocks. From old wishbones to pens that don't work, leave it to the art teacher to repurpose and reuse!

I once organized an art studio for a former art teacher. I should say that I *created* an art studio for her because what we started with was a room filled to the ceiling with art supplies. I was there to help her bring to life her dream of creating an art studio, but first we had to empty the room of its contents and find out what we could reasonably store in the room. As we began the process of emptying the space, we began to discuss what could go and what had to stay in the studio. I quickly learned that the client loathed the idea of getting rid of anything. She argued that her supplies were "still good" and "could be used again" although they hadn't been touched in years. She kept referring to how her students would use up the supplies even though she was no longer a teacher! I pointed out that the supplies could be donated to local schools, where active teachers would be thankful to have the material. From the look on her face, I could tell that was not going to happen.

We both agreed that the new art studio would not hold all of the supplies she was storing in there because she needed access and work space. She had originally told me that a lot of the material would be thrown away or given away, but when the time arrived, she just couldn't face parting with her chaotic classroom. Between appointments with me, she stealthily began moving the mass of supplies into her bedroom, her office, and the family room. Upon my return, I could see that she was territorial about her belongings and that she was not about to be separated from her art supplies. She would rather bury her other rooms with art supplies than part with one paint brush. Much to my chagrin, prolific art supplies from her storage room began creeping all over the house like the spread of disease!

The reason to cut out deadwood from a plant is to open it up and ensure healthy circulation of air and energy. The art teacher didn't have useless stuff, but she certainly had too much stuff. Her crowded space was like a tangled tree with crossing branches and clumps of rotting foliage. If she had been willing to cut out the deadwood from her supplies and pull out the excess, she could have contained her items to the art studio and prevented her stuff from spreading like disease. Sometimes people behold their excessive belongings, receive a much-needed reality check, and begin to let go of the surplus. Others hold on to their excess belongings indefinitely and live in a constant state of overkill that chokes out healthy living.

Opportunity Cost

Before you think that all an organizer does is try to make you get rid of your belongings, I want to clarify. My purpose is never to force someone to throw something away or give it to a worthy cause. People often have very good reasons for wanting to keep their sentimental belongings, collections, and supplies. We acknowledge and honor everyone's right to keep the things that make them feel good and safe. Yet many of the things people want to keep are either no longer serving them or are stored away where no one can enjoy them.

A good organizer will help you assess your priorities and the opportunity cost of keeping your items. "Opportunity cost" is a term I've lifted from the world of economics, and I'm using it to mean the trade-offs you will pay to keep an item. If you save it, you will have to find a home for it, group it, store it, label it, dust it, insure it, and find it again! Because you are keeping some items, you may not have room to keep other items. If you've evaluated the opportunity cost of keeping an item and decided that it is worth saving, then you can feel confident that you have made a thoughtful choice. The reason many people accumulate too much stuff is that they just keep everything instead of taking the time to evaluate the opportunity cost of keeping each item.

Come to Terms with Your Calendar

We can take a good hard look at our calendar and begin thatching out the deadwood there too. Recently, I met with a CEO who is excessively busy. He was fascinated by the concept of a professional organizer, and he knew that he wanted one in his life. Even with an executive assistant and a personal assistant, he needed help managing all the complexity that goes along with work, office obligations, social activities, and altruistic ventures.

Before long, he confided to me that he was on the board of directors of 16 different organizations! He admitted that he couldn't keep up with the mission and activities of so many organizations. We had formed an easy friendship, so I laughed out loud. "How in the world are you managing that?" I asked incredulously. He laughed too and confessed with a smile, "Not very well!"

As we began working together, we focused on determining his priorities. We are in the process of identifying the activities and organizations that add meaning and purpose to his life and those that are simply obligations. We have already identified and are beginning to phase out activities that are choking his schedule with unnecessary duty. Our goal is to bring some sanity and purpose back into his life.

As a dead branch saps energy from the tree, senseless activity drains energy from our lives. If you find yourself drowning in events, meetings, clubs, teams, and activities, now is the time to begin cutting out the excess! By cutting out that which is useless or unnecessary, we save more energy for the things that truly matter.

Saying No

Some people are afraid to end their obligations and commitments. They fear how the other board members will react if they exit their role. The overcommitted wonder how their committees and groups will get along without them if they quit, even though they know they are not giving any of their groups their full attention because they are too busy. The overprogrammed masses have succumbed to pressure by others and even their own sincere desires, resulting in an insane schedule.

Most of us are too busy for our own good—including me sometimes. No one wants to lose face or let others down. However, guilt or obligation should never drive our commitments. Our priorities should drive our commitments.

Your overrun schedule can actually begin to suffocate your quality of life. Excess stuff and too many commitments deplete our energy and time. Saying no is the place to start cutting out the deadwood.

Trim Back the Good Stuff

Eliminating superfluous, burdensome stuff and obligations in order to live healthier, more productive lives makes good sense. Once we've cut out the deadwood from our space and our time, can we stop there? Savvy gardeners know that removing dead stuff from foliage is necessary and pruning back living plants will cause a garden to flourish. In fact, if a plant isn't thriving, pruning will give it a fresh new start.

Pruning Forces Resiliency

This isn't the first year that Trevor hacked back our hydrangeas. Before his first garden rampage, my hydrangeas were spindly and woody. The too-long branches became weighed down with the big bouquets of blooms. When a hard rain pounded the yard, the branches splayed out, heavy with water. They looked kind of pathetic. After Trevor chops them back each year, their energy returns to the base, and I've noticed that year after year the base has become sturdier. Through pruning, he has forced some resiliency into those hydrangeas, and now their branches stand up tall and stout, withstanding wind and rainstorms like tight-knit soldiers.

Yearly pruning has instilled a sturdiness that was lacking before.

Organizations, like gardens, sometimes need pruning when they are not thriving. I sit on a board of directors for a local rescue mission for the homeless. Recently, our income wasn't meeting our needs, and we were forced to make some cuts. We couldn't see any "fat" that could be cut back. However, our financial committee gave the board instructions to cut several positions in both the men's and women's ministries. The directive seemed so unfair. Why couldn't we just raise more money to meet the growing needs? Why did we have to cut back?

A month later, we met as a board with the leadership team of the two ministries to discuss the effects of the cutbacks. I was prepared to hear reports about disgruntled and devastated employees and how fewer hands were doing more work. As we sat down at the table, the respective leaders were beaming. Each of the ministries reported some amazing results of their cutbacks.

At the women's ministry, every person whose position was eliminated offered to donate their time as a volunteer! Creative solutions to cover the necessary work resulted in a new job schedule that now included the clients. Formerly homeless women were learning life and vocational skills they never would have received without the cutbacks!

At the men's ministry, a revised employee schedule allowed the workers to move among the homeless guests as they could never do before. They became more hands-on and started having more authentic interactions and conversations with the guests. The employees and the clients were formerly two groups, separated by their life circumstances, and now they were merging back into the human family with real relationships.

Cutbacks, we all learned, can release creativity and flexibility to meet needs. Trimming the budget forced this ministry to become resourceful and resilient. The mission's willingness to go through the process of pruning allowed it to thrive again.

Pruning Focuses Energy

Our hydrangeas not only became more resilient with pruning, they became stronger and sturdier too. By cutting off living stock, the nutrients were forced back into the base of the plant. Pruning back even the good things in our life can redirect our energy and resources to the core of our personal and professional life.

In the first year of my exploding organizing business, I sat bawling in front of my computer. I was overwhelmed to the point of tears. Have you ever been totally overwhelmed because you had too many responsibilities? Beside me was a huge pile of receipts. I had my financial software program open, and I was doing grindingly slow data entry. I knew I had to force myself to do this dreaded task. Or did I?

My skills are in leadership, communication, and execution, not in data entry! I finally realized that this function of the business had to be done, but not by me. I had skills and gifts that I needed to use, but I was sitting in front of my computer instead of generating business. Immediately I hired a bookkeeper and outsourced that function of my business. I cut the role of bookkeeper off my job description in order to make more time for working in my strengths.

As my new bookkeeper took over this data entry role, I could begin to think strategically and analytically about the company's finances. Now she generates weekly and monthly reports for me with key indicators that I want to see. We scheduled a monthly financial review, and I began to become the chief financial officer that I could never be when I was doing the bookkeeping. Trimming back my job description allowed my key roles to emerge.

What tasks or roles in your personal or professional life should you prune back? Is your housework draining all the time you could be investing in starting a new business? Is an unfulfilling career stealing time from your parenting? Are you spending every weekend maintaining your yard while your dreams sit on the back burner? We all have to do some things we don't like doing, but sometimes we can get someone else to do those things we don't enjoy or have time for.

Now, before you think I'm suggesting that the only answer is to hire a maid, nanny, or gardener and selfishly focus on yourself, hold on to your pruners. What I am suggesting is that we get brave, like those at the mission, and cut back some stuff in our lives so we can make room for the things that really matter to us.

The purpose of pruning is to allow us to be even more fruitful and productive in our lives (remember John 15:1-2?). If you were to prune back your budget, you might force more creative use of family funds. Instead of dinners out on the town, you may actually discover romantic dinners at home. If you pruned back your chores, you might find that enlisting your kids' help actually transfers some much-needed life skills to them and raises their accountability. If you cut back your work responsibilities to focus your energy on your slipping parenting, you may find that a job share was the perfect balance between work and home. The point is this: Unless we are willing to question the roles and activities in our life and expose them to pruning, we may never experience the fruit on the other side of the pruners.

Pruning Produces New Life

The most obvious result of pruning is the new life that springs forth from the trimmed stalks. Here in Oregon, roses will bloom practically all summer if you keep cutting them back. Annual flowers like pansies and petunias will continue producing their glorious and prolific blooms if you pinch back their spent blooms and some of their stems. Like many things in life, pruning is an ongoing maintenance habit that produces new life.

Organizing is a lot like pruning. Simplifying your space and schedule will invigorate your life. I've found that when our clients get serious about pulling out that which is superfluous and paring down even the good things in their lives, they are able to experience more freedom. They begin living their true priorities.

Vines or branches that trail off from the plant distract energy from the source. The excess stuff and obligations in our lives also distract us from our key roles and purposes. Pruning back good stalk creates healthier, rejuvenated plants that are more resilient. The new life is better prepared to fight off disease and withstand storms. In the same way, when we trim back our belongings and our commitments, we free up our own energy to focus on the important things in life. By cutting back, we revitalize ourselves!

Pruning Trains Growth

Christmas trees are big business here in Oregon, and our farmers ship them all over the country. These gorgeous trees do not develop their beautiful shape by accident; the tree farmer proactively trains the tree's growth in direction and form. He prunes off stray branches to create the coned appearance. He cuts off the lower branches to maintain the height he wants. Just as the tree farmer shapes desirable Christmas trees, we can shape the life we desire by regularly pruning our environment and time.

You can use the Pruning Principle to eliminate deadwood from your environment and time and to cut back even the good things in your life to produce resiliency, focus, and new life. Ever notice how your stuff takes on a life of its own? When toys start to multiply like rabbits and paper begins to morph all over the house, the time has come to get out the pruners and take control. Even your schedule can begin to take over your life, and like the excessively busy CEO, you can find yourself overcommitted. No one can take back your time but you, and it can only happen when you begin pulling the meaningless obligations out of your calendar and trimming back even your sensible activities.

Lastly, you can use the Pruning Principle to control future growth—to evaluate the addition of new belongings and new opportunities into your life. When you work hard to eliminate deadwood and pare back your belongings and calendar, you will also become cautious about adding anything new into your life. After you've applied the Pruning Principle and stimulated your life, you will want to protect your newfound freedom!

11

The Possibility Principle

I shared earlier that people change because of priorities, pain, or possibility. In this chapter, we will discuss how possibility can act as a catalyst for you to get organized.

Many of us are distracted by our disorder and cannot see the possibilities for our life. Instead of discovering the fullness of our capabilities and passions, we are stuck in a holding pattern of confusion in our cluttered homes and offices. If we cannot see possibilities, we get lodged in a rut and lose hope. Instead of moving forward, we stagnate in our personal and professional lives. If we would invest the time to order our space and our lives, we would bring possibilities into focus, meet our potential, and enjoy a higher quality of life.

The Possibility Principle is this: When we engage in organizing, we reclaim our potential, embrace possibilities, and enhance our quality of life. A lifestyle of order liberates us to serve others and live on purpose. Get ready to be inspired to trade in your disorganization for possibility!

Reclaim Your Potential

Sharon runs a direct-sales clothing business from her home office. She also has a full-time job, so she works on her business during limited hours in the evenings and on weekends. Like all sole proprietors, she is the chief executive officer as well as the janitor! Every day she juggles a myriad of tasks including marketing, sales, and financial management. Keeping all of her roles straight is hard for Sharon. With so much on her plate, she isn't providing the kind of customer service that maximizes awareness and keeps customers coming back.

As an independent businessperson, Sharon must ensure her own productivity because she doesn't have a boss checking in on her. She would love to increase her income, but her sales are not what she had hoped they would be because she is disorganized. Her home office is overwhelming to her and represents the convergence of her personal and professional life. From personal bills to customer spreadsheets to memorabilia, her desk is covered with layers of paper. She is like a lot of home-based business owners who haven't created separate systems for their home and work life; her productivity is stymied by her chaos.

Because Sharon doesn't have the systems she needs to run her business effectively, she is distracted by her disorder. When she sits down at her desk, she can't even think. Sometimes her disorganization actually prevents her from getting started. Instead of working on high-priority tasks like planning sales parties or calling customers, she spends an hour tidying her work space so she can think more clearly. Suddenly, her short window of opportunity to work on her business has disappeared, and she must return to home life.

Other times, Sharon uses her disorganization as an excuse to procrastinate on tasks she should be doing. To notify her customers about new products, Sharon needs to be sending mailings and calling customers on the phone. If she isn't moving product, she isn't making money. Instead, Sharon spends time on lower-priority tasks (like arranging office supplies) rather than income-generating activities. She reasons that she will get to the higher-priority tasks just as soon as she gets organized.

Sharon dreams of having someone else tackle the paperwork and data entry for her so she can focus on making sales. Unfortunately, she hasn't achieved a high volume of sales yet, and though she detests the details associated with her business, she can't afford to hire an assistant. The paradox is that until Sharon gets systems in place and gets organized, she can't achieve the sales results she feels she would need in order to hire someone to get her organized!

Sharon has two choices: She can remain in her disorder and keep up a minimal level of sales, or she can resolve to address her disorder and equip herself for professional success. Sharon is not without hope because she is entirely aware of her self-defeating habits. She knows that her disorganization is keeping her from making more sales and increasing her income. She is clear that her disorganization is costing her customers as she loses leads and opportunities expire. Sharon even understands that she is avoiding the problem, and as a result her disorganization grows.

Pain is a factor for Sharon but not how you might expect. Sharon is not facing much external pain from her disorganization. She doesn't have a boss who is disappointed in her performance. Her customers don't even know about the new products that are in stock, so they're not let down by her lack of communication. Even her customers that are not receiving great service aren't complaining; they are just quietly going away. Sharon's pain is internal because she alone knows how much better she could do.

The internal pain Sharon experiences manifests itself in frustration and lower self-esteem. She needs a reason bigger than her internal pain to get organized. Her day job pays the bills, but Sharon wants to add to her family's income. Most importantly, she wants to prove to herself that she can make her business profitable. As she evaluates her two choices, Sharon decides to get equipped for success. She is inspired by the possibilities that lie ahead for her and commits to getting organized.

Reclaim Your Quality of Life

Conventional wisdom defines organizing as "a place for everything and everything in its place." In my view, organizing is about so much more than finding a home for things. Organizing is not about simply finding, storing, and labeling things. Living in order allows you to operate at your full potential, which liberates you to invest in your true priorities. Quite simply, being organized enhances your quality of work and life. As you begin to order your space and your life, you will have more time to invest in yourself, in others, and in your dreams.

Invest in Yourself

Deirdre hired me because she was drowning at work. She is a financial planner who needed to improve her work flow.

Paper piles were causing her angst, and she couldn't find anything. Her business was doing quite well, and her clients were happy with the service she was providing. But when we spoke, Deirdre looked tired and worn down by her own success!

As we went through her intake assessment, I learned that she was an avid gardener. In fact, she would rather garden than work. She just loved getting her hands in the dirt and watching vegetables and flowers spring up. She also loved restoring old furniture to its original glory. As her business grew, Deirdre began to have less and less time for gardening and scouring garage sales for furniture.

Together, we discovered that one of Deirdre's priorities was to make time for herself. She needed to get away from her thriving financial planning business and rejuvenate by enjoying her hobbies. She couldn't go on at her frenetic pace without a respite much longer.

We set up systems for Deirdre to manage the onslaught of paper across her desk. We overhauled her filing system and created categories for easy reference where none existed before. We organized her paper, office supplies, and forms. Once all Deirdre's new systems were in place, I trained her assistant how to use them.

Finally, Deirdre got her entire team together, and I worked with all six people to define their job descriptions. One key step to get Deirdre organized was limiting the tasks she was managing and delegating some of those tasks to others. Understanding Deirdre's systems was essential for her team.

Even if you have taken the time to establish good systems, you may still be overloaded with more than one person can reasonably accomplish. Sometimes we feel disorganized simply because we have taken on too much responsibility. If you need to pare down your job description, you can recruit others to share your tasks so that you have more time to work in your strengths.

Like Deirdre, we all need to invest in ourselves in order to reclaim our quality of life. If our personal fuel tank is running on empty, we will soon burn out. Investing in yourself may include establishing orderly systems to operate more effectively at work and at home. It may also include offloading tasks that you cannot manage anymore. Finally, investing in yourself involves spending time enjoying your hobbies and relaxing. When you are refueled, you will have more to give at home and at work.

If you left your hobbies somewhere in the distant past and you find yourself running at mach speed, then you and I have something in common! For me, the hardest part of reclaiming my quality of life is giving myself free time. I don't really have many hobbies other than scrapbooking, which I rarely make time for in my schedule. Instead of hobbies, my commitment to myself is to plan dinners out with friends and an occasional spa treatment.

I color-code my calendar, and my personal "refueling" activities are purple. I try to have at least one personal activity per week I can look forward to. Weddings to attend and even group activities aren't always marked purple. I only mark those activities that will offer personal respite with the color purple. If you have a hard time investing in yourself, don't take up a hobby if it just seems like more work! Think about the activities that bring you simple pleasure and the people with whom you want to stay connected, and begin scheduling those activities and times with those people! Investing in yourself will help you reclaim your life. As you refuel, the possibilities that lie ahead will begin to come into focus.

Invest in Others

Recently I was speaking to a group about organizing their work flow. After the engagement, Tammy approached me and shared with me that she was so embarrassed about her cluttered household that she no longer invited people over to visit. She was ashamed of her mess, and she told me that she simply had to get her home organized so she could get rid of her shame. She felt bad that her home was no longer a place for people to gather.

When our disorganization compromises our quality of life, we sometimes allow it to alienate us from our social life. Instead of feeling free to invite people over, or even go out with others, we feel obligated to stay home and take care of our problem. The same thing happens at work. If our clutter is piling up around us, we hunker down and skip lunches, keep our door closed, and stay later to try to get ahead of our mess. As we become more separated from others and more stressed about our disorder, our quality of life suffers.

Invest in Your Dreams

Some of us won't feel as if we are meeting our potential or enjoying quality of life unless we are pursuing our dreams. My dream is to grow a national brand of life management. I've truly found my calling in life, and every day I am blessed to do what I love for a living. If I didn't pursue my dream, I would be letting myself down. Having met so many people who dislike their careers, I recognize how rarely people live their dreams. Most people wish they could rearrange their life to get their dreams off the back burner. I tell them that with a little sweat equity they can do just that!

Investing in my dreams doesn't come without sacrifice. I have taken the time to set up systems at home and at work that keep my space, time, and paper in order. I keep an eye on those systems and adapt them as my needs change. I have a more modest social calendar than my friends have. I don't have children yet. I put in a lot more hours at the office than most people I know. I pay a lot of people to help carry my load in my professional and personal life. With my money committed to uphold my business and home life, I have less money for vacations or huge savings accounts. I trade in some things other people have in order to fulfill my calling. My sacrifices are really just trade-offs. For me, investing in my dreams is a key element in enjoying quality of life.

I never want to look back and wonder what would have happened if I would have had the guts or money or time to go after my dreams. I can live without regrets because I know that I am right where I should be; I am investing in my God-given calling and in my dreams!

Reclaim Your Service

Remember Sharon's direct-sales clothing business? She decided to hire a professional organizer to get help establishing systems to run her business. In the process, she also learned what to do with all her personal paper. She set up a bill-paying system and created a method for capturing and storing memorabilia. As she established her systems and began to use them faithfully, she no longer dreaded entering her home office. The few hours she had dedicated to her business each week grew into a few more hours because she started to enjoy working! She launched mailings on a regular basis, and her clients began calling her to see if she could introduce the clothing to their friends. Sharon's business was picking up speed!

Once Sharon simplified her environment and created her business systems, she could focus on her true passion: helping others. As she cleared her space and mind of clutter, she rediscovered her heart for service.

As Sharon started meeting more people, she realized that what her customers really wanted was an improved self-image. As her home parties grew more popular, Sharon responded to this need by inviting an image consultant to the parties to talk about inner and outer beauty. She also developed a directory of service providers that would meet her clients' needs in related areas. She was reenergized to serve her customers' spoken and unspoken needs. Her customers began to see Sharon as a resource, and they felt proud to refer her to their friends.

When we are serving others, we benefit as well because we feel good about making a contribution. Working for our ego or our financial benefit feels pretty empty. When our work serves a higher purpose, however, we add meaning and purpose to others' lives as well as our own. When you are living your calling and serving others, you are giving back some of what you've received. If you would like to release service and impact others with your life, begin investing in order to realize your full potential!

Live Intentionally

Sharon, Deirdre, and Tammy all had something in common. Their disorganization was preventing them from living the way they wanted to live. Each of these women felt guilty about the things she wasn't doing. Sharon was buried in confusion and wasn't serving her customers. Deirdre wasn't taking care of herself and was running out of steam. Tammy wasn't enjoying her friends and family due to her shame about her messy space. Instead of recognizing and seizing possibilities in their lives, these women were stuck in a self-defeating cycle.

When we are not doing the things that are important to us, we aren't living in congruence with our values. When we are out of sync with our own values, we experience anxiety and self-condemnation. Living out our life priorities with direction and purpose is difficult when we are occupied with surviving (or avoiding!) the chaos. We feel restricted by our chaos, and we want to know how to take back control. We are tired of living under the weight of our burden of disorder. We can't be true to ourselves and our priorities when we are driven by guilt or anxiety or shame. When we take the time to bring our space and life into orderly focus, we can live our lives the way we intend to.

When our professional organizers sit down with new clients, we don't hear a sterile analysis of the disorganization they are facing; we hear the affects of the disorder on their life! People pour out their frustrations with themselves and their family members or coworkers. They bemoan all that they are not doing that they know they could be accomplishing. They talk about being overwhelmed and guilty and pained. We hear examples of what their disorder is costing their home and work life; they are losing relationships and promotions and confidence.

Our clients have taught us that people aren't as frustrated with disorganization itself as they are frustrated with the impact of their disorganization on their life. For this very reason, overly simplistic tips that address the mess itself are unlikely to work. We need to address the life impact of our disorganization in order to get inspired to change.

We feel free when we live with intention and purpose each day. What would your life look like if you lived intentionally? Would you have a different attitude about your day? Would different people and activities fill your calendar? Would you let go of some superfluous commitments in order to enjoy your true priorities? How could you strive each day to fulfill your potential? How would your quality of life change if you could get organized? If you've been thwarted by your disorganization, you can reclaim your potential and quality of life when you choose to get organized. You will find more time to serve, and your influence and impact on others will grow. When you get organized, you are choosing to live with intention.

Part Three

Organizing Strategies

12

Dig Out and Dig In

Michael and Tim are managing business partners in a 12-person law firm. Each is disorganized in his own way.

Michael is historically and habitually disorganized. His parents never taught him to organize his space and his life. As a result, he developed bad habits that contribute to his disorganization. Clutter has followed him his whole life. From job to job and even relationship to relationship, Michael has carried the baggage of disorder. Like many of his previous offices, his current office is buried under piles of paper. He works so many hours he hardly ever leaves the office. He spends more time at work than at home. He pays his personal bills and does his taxes at the office. Michael even keeps food and a change of clothes at his office!

In a law firm, time is measured by the billable hour, and hours are the only thing a services firm has to sell. For as hard as Michael works and as many hours as he puts into his job, he doesn't bill that many hours. Why? Michael is disorganized with his time as well as with his paper. Plenty of phone calls and hallway conversations with associates never get recorded as billable time. Michael's mind is full of clutter, and he forgets to write down the calls and conversations. As a result, he freely gives his clients a huge sum of potentially billable time. Because the firm makes less income, Michael has to work even harder and longer hours to keep the firm afloat. His bad habit of not capturing his time is contributing to his mad cycle of work.

As a managing partner, Michael is also supposed to dedicate time to actually managing his staff. This is difficult for him because he has a hard time capturing, processing, and retrieving all the paper associated with his growing firm. Papers disappear into the vortex of his office, never to be seen again. Michael would like to take a leadership role to ensure accountability from his staff and to mentor less experienced attorneys. However, he can't keep track of the papers and action items that come from management and staff meetings, so supervising and training his staff is out of the question for now.

Michael uses one of those huge desktop paper calendars. He tears off the month when it is finished—at least that is what he is supposed to do. Michael's calendar is a few months behind, and he doesn't want to toss old pages because they contain valuable information. The calendar is covered in coffee stains, phone numbers, and notes to self. The calendar doesn't really work for him, but he reasons that he doesn't have time to figure out a different system. From paper to time management, Michael needs help to dig out of his disorganized office.

Tim is situationally and habitually disorganized, although he is actually a pretty organized person at home. Back when he and Michael struck out on their own and started the firm, he had good systems in place to maintain order. As the more organized of the two, Tim was forced to take on the management role that Michael wasn't fulfilling. This required more hours and paperwork and tasks in addition to serving his own clients. Files and spreadsheets began to populate his desktop in layers on a regular basis. His situation with his business partner forced him into taking on too many responsibilities and that precipitated his decline of order.

Tim is a natural business developer. He has power lunches and meet-and-greets where he sells the firm's services. He speaks at industry events and associations. His speaking activities require additional scheduling, tasks, and paperwork. These business development tasks contribute to Tim's overwhelmed feeling at work. Although he enjoys developing business, he is considering stopping speaking altogether so he can focus on his backlog of paperwork and tasks.

Tim has settled into the bad habit of avoidance. Unlike Michael, who is always in the office, Tim tries to schedule himself out of the office. He hates to accept the state of chaos in his office because it conflicts with his natural need for order. He reasons that he needs to be out generating business anyway; after all, someone has to do it. By putting off the pain he faces in his office, he is not getting any closer to resolving it.

The good news is that both Michael and Tim want to change. They hired me to evaluate their respective offices and begin a transformation. I made appointments with each of them, and we began our organizing journey. Michael had never experienced an orderly life, so he really wanted to change his space and his habits. Tim longed to restore order to his practice and to his life.

Michael made a series of appointments with me, and we dove into his project with enthusiasm. His assessment took a while because his office actually represented the convergence of all his business and personal systems in one space. His priority was to clear his desk, which he thought shouldn't take very long. However, we had to touch every piece of paper and make a decision about it. This was painful for Michael because he had set each piece aside precisely because he didn't know how to process it! Answering questions about his paper and finally making decisions was grindingly painful for him. During that first appointment, we were able, however, to set up a center for him to process paper. He still had a long way to go, but this was a start.

Soon after, Michael called me to reschedule our next appointment. He said the time we had spent together was incredibly valuable, but now he was even further behind and needed a week to catch up. A month passed before I got Michael back on my calendar, and we pressed on. I noticed that the same papers that were in his processing center a month previous were still sitting in the trays. He hadn't touched them. When I asked him if he had a chance to process his paper, he seemed defeated. Michael acted helpless about his disorganization and continued to operate in his foxhole of disorder. His pain appeared to be more acute than his commitment.

Tim also made a series of appointments with me, but he booked back-to-back dates. He wanted to concentrate our efforts to make rapid progress. Energy bars in hand, I welcomed the challenge, and together we powered through his assessment in a short time. His pace was faster than Michael's, but I could also see a different level of commitment from him.

I could read in his face that failure was not an option. He wanted to restore order so badly he dedicated three billable days to his organizing project.

Today, one attorney is organized, and one is not. Who do you think persevered? If you guessed Tim, you are correct. Tim did his due diligence and is reaping the benefits. Michael still wants to get organized, and occasionally he and I get together to make more progress. He has seen Tim soar with reestablished order and wants the same outcome for himself.

Yet Michael isn't willing to carve out the necessary time to get momentum on his project. Even though Michael probably wastes hours a day in inefficiencies and searching for documents, he can't make the connection between the investment in organizing and his professional effectiveness. Until he dedicates the necessary time to setting up good systems for paper and time management, he will continue to waste his time.

We all come to a point where we have to make a decision. We have only two options: Either we stay in our pain or we take action to extricate ourselves from the pain by getting through the Pain Tunnel. When someone makes a partial commitment or lacks follow-through for whatever reason, they may be only counting the cost of their organizing venture. However, when someone makes a total commitment and follows through on their intentions, they are paying the piper in order to reap the dividends.

Counting the Cost

Did Michael's process fall short because he didn't dedicate back-to-back days on his project? It's hard to tell. We definitely would have made faster progress if he had. The momentum itself would have motivated Michael. Still,

Michael could have simply kept his series of appointments and made steady progress in periodic visits. Did Michael need more time or did he need more commitment? Probably both.

When we count the cost of getting organized, we can find dozens of reasons why we can't go forward with our projects. We worry we might fail. We wonder how our life or career will change if we actually succeed. We hate to part with our valuable time. We can think of a lot of other things we'd rather be doing. We want to avoid the pain of decisions and hard work. Some of our reasons might have validity. Others are just excuses. At some point, however, we must decide whether we are going to continue counting the cost or take the plunge into change.

I'm not a counselor qualified to diagnose psychological behavior, but I can tell you what I see in the field. I have observed that often those who count up all the perceived costs of getting organized actually *create* the results they fear. They worry their efforts won't last, so they don't fully commit to the organizing process. Because they don't embrace the process, they fulfill their own prophecy. When I hear a client say, "I just don't think I'll have the time to maintain order once I get organized," I know that they are projecting a fear into the future. They use this fear as a reason not to get started. Instead of projecting your fears and counting the costs of an investment in organizing, you can resolve to dig in and pay the piper.

Paying the Piper

If Tim had taken a slower approach to tackling his messy office, would he have been less successful? I doubt it. Tim had the courage and commitment necessary to stare down his disorganization and conquer it. Tim had reached a point of pain, a point of reckoning. Instead of wallowing in pain, he decided to dig out and move on.

Paying the piper requires you to face the consequences for your past disorganization once and for all so that you can claim your freedom from the prison of disorder. It is stepping up to the plate and owning your situation. It is agreeing not to turn back in the middle of the Pain Tunnel but going all the way through it. Paying the piper means doing whatever is necessary for you to dig out. It means sacrificing some things temporarily in order to achieve your long-term goals.

As you begin, you will need to cover two important bases if you want your efforts to last. Your organizing process won't work unless you tackle backlog and set up systems for managing your life.

Tackling backlog means that you must *dig out* of the accumulated possessions or paper or tasks that you've collected. Setting up systems means that you need to *dig in* and establish structure to ensure that your disorder doesn't return. Both are necessary steps. If you dig out of your mess but don't set up systems, you won't be able to create order in your future. If you dig in and set up systems but don't deal with your backlog, it will infiltrate your systems.

Dig Out

Backlog

To dig out of your disorganization, you will need to deal with backlog. Backlog is the years or months or days of accumulation. It is anything you haven't done that is cluttering your environment or your to-do list. It has probably been hanging around for a long time, and you've been avoiding it. You know what I'm talking about...it's in your basement, your office closet, and your kitchen cabinets.

Backlog isn't just comprised of stuff; it can also be made up of our tasks and responsibilities. My task list is huge! If I am out of the office consulting or traveling for a period of time, I have less bandwidth to attend to administrative tasks in the office. When I return, I face an exploding to-do list. Even if I am in the office working diligently, my business goes through phases where demand increases, and my tasks ramp up with the workload.

Part of digging out is committing to processing your tasks and belongings on a consistent basis. Until I have a catch-up day, my backlog of tasks picks up volume and speed! Don't get me wrong; I still do maintenance activities even when I'm busy out of the office or with increased demand. But if I'm not diligent to process my papers and responsibilities every single day and devote additional longer periods to catching up, I would be overcome by backlog. Even a professional organizer has to deal with backlog!

Obviously, you can't really dig out of your disorganization without a commitment of time. You'll have to pay the piper with your time. Your time is indeed valuable, but if you invest it in your own organization process, you will reap the benefits. If you are willing to invest some time, you can exchange your disorganization for a higher quality of life.

When we are organizing, we need time to make all those decisions that we've put off for so long. This is one of the reasons we subconsciously postpone our projects. Even though our home or office may desperately need our attention, we know that once we get started, we will have to face a plethora of time-consuming decisions. We are programmed to conduct our lives at a rapid rate, so we naturally resist anything that is time-consuming. Organizing is time-consuming, but it is an investment in quality of life.

Like Michael, many people don't want to dedicate time to organizing because they are afraid, they are delaying pain, or they are skeptical. If you want to dig out, you'll need to set aside a block of time to your projects.

Dump the Deadwood

Remember the Pruning Principle? Now is the time to apply it! As you deal with backlog, you will run across things you don't need, don't use, don't like, or that don't serve your purposes anymore. You will have the opportunity to grab the deadwood and yank it out. Superfluous stuff in your space and schedule is no longer safe! Empowered by your commitment to your quality of life, you can get out the pruners and start chopping out the unnecessary stuff that is clogging up your life.

Some people like the rule that if you haven't used something within a year, let it go. Personally, my broad rule of thumb is that if the object doesn't serve a utilitarian purpose or add beauty or meaning to your life, you can dump it. Certainly, that doesn't mean that you should toss things without thinking, but you can evaluate each item using my standard or a standard of your own.

Don't forget that you can dump the deadwood in your schedule too. Thin out the extraneous activities and tasks. Extricate yourself from overcommitment. Simplify your calendar by starting with your basic responsibilities and adding only what is truly necessary and enriching. I've found that color-coding my calendar allows me to achieve more balance. Green represents financial activities, grey specifies administrative activities, red indicates client activities, orange codes spiritual activities, purple distinguishes personal activities, and so on. As I look at my colorful schedule, I can see where I have too much of one type of activity or a paucity of another. Taking the time to organize your calendar and limit your commitments will help you recapture time for the things you enjoy.

Dig In

As you invest time to assault backlog, you will purge stuff you don't need anymore. As you emerge from your prison of disorder, you will want to do anything you can to keep the order you've created. To maintain your simplified spaces, you'll need to set up systems for going forward.

Establish Systems

Every adult has to deal with paper. We receive a flood of paper every day. From junk mail to work projects to reading material, paper is inescapable. Even in this age of digital imaging, we will always need a way to manage paper in some form.

Every office needs at least three paper-management systems. First, you need a way to capture incoming, actionable paper. A method of processing and advancing paper will keep those nasty piles off your surfaces. Second, you need a place to store pending projects. Whether you're undertaking a remodel or working on a client transaction, a project cannot be done in one step. Eventually, your remodel or transaction will be complete, and you can move documents into the third necessary paper-management system: permanent reference. Everyone needs a useful filing system with simple categories and labels. Most of us have years of deadwood in our file drawers that we can expunge. The purpose of a filing system is to store paper you will need to reference again. You have many different kinds of paper, so you need distinct systems for managing the various types.

Some people want to address their backlog of paper but don't know how to set up systems for effective paper management. They may spend an entire weekend at the office tossing out old files and shredding sensitive documents. By the end of their weekend, they feel fabulous. They have reclaimed their office—or so they thought. Weeks or perhaps just days later, their mess returns like the plague. They are disillusioned with the organizing process, and they feel defeated once again. Why did the mess return? Without introducing *systems* for managing incoming paper, the backlog will return in a hurry. Digging out, in other words, will only last if you dig in and initiate structures for handling your paper and belongings in the future.

I've given my employees a mantra for our organizing method: Do it right, do it custom, and do it once! If you want your organizing systems to last, follow our mantra when instituting structures for dealing with your paper, time, and space.

"Do it right" means that your systems will succeed only when you have taken the time to think through the issues, create a plan, and apply a discovery process. Doing it wrong would be haphazardly attacking one part without considering the whole picture. Identify which systems you will need in each space and set them up. Get help if you don't know where to start.

"Do it custom" means making sure that you are taking your own unique needs, lifestyle, and preferences into account. If you apply a cookie-cutter solution, you will have to train yourself in someone else's thinking. Personalize your systems by setting them up in an intuitive, simple manner. Resist overcomplicating things.

Finally, if you've applied our mantra, you should only have to "do it once." Tired of organizing and reorganizing? You may have had to try and try again because you haven't engaged in a thorough discovery process or customized your systems.

Go the Distance

Tim, the attorney who restored order to his life, not only paid the piper but also made the investment some are afraid to make. Like a steely-eyed runner at the start of a marathon, he mentally committed to finish the race. He put his secretary on notice that he was unavailable for three days. He directed his office phone and cell phone to voice mail. Tim went the distance. If you want to achieve lasting results like Tim's, you will have to go the distance.

If your organizing project is short and contained, you may not need the kind of endurance that a longer, more complex project would require. If you only have a closet or desktop that needs organizing, you can block out the necessary time and go for it. However, many people have multiple rooms or an entire office that needs attention. They will need more stamina.

Train yourself by organizing something small first, like a bathroom. Engage in a discovery process and examine the costs and causes of your disorganization. Tackle the backlog. Implement the necessary systems to prevent clutter from accumulating in the future. Keep your energy by drinking or eating when necessary. Promise yourself a reward when you finish the bathroom, like going for a long, refreshing walk, and focus on your reward as you work through your project. Remind yourself of all the benefits you will experience when your bathroom is organized, like cruising through a smoother morning routine and avoiding buying too many products. Don't forget to celebrate by enjoying your reward!

Total Burn Down

Imelda is a client who had a terribly disorganized multi-purpose room. It served as a closet, dressing room, guest room, and home office. Clothes and papers and books and gifts were strewed everywhere.

When she hired me to organize the space, I was surprised by her goals. She had no intention of limiting the purposes of the room. The four other closets in the house were unrelated in her mind, and she really didn't want to curb her shopaholic habits. She wanted me to tidy up the room and help her donate some clothes she no longer liked.

I tried in vain to explain to her that if she didn't simplify the purposes of the room, she would continue to deal with the convergence of all these activities in one space. I recommended we set up a useful home office elsewhere in the home so we could dedicate work space and file space to eliminate the paper piles. I also pointed out that we could consolidate her closets and create two seasonal closets with some serious purging. I did the best I could to help Imelda, pointing out along the way the systems that she needed for long-term success. She thanked me for my ideas but clearly had no desire to implement them.

Imelda really wasn't interested in a long-term solution; she was looking for a Band-Aid. Sure enough, when I called to check in on Imelda six months later, she complained that her clothes and paper had again taken over the room. She said she just didn't have the motivation to try again because the first attempt didn't work.

Imelda had made several organizing mistakes. One error was that she only scratched the surface of her disorganization by tidying up the space. She neither dug out of backlog nor set up systems for going forward. For lasting success, she would have had to tackle all the contributing factors to the disorder evidenced in this room. A useful organizing process would have included establishing distinct locations for the guest room, the home office, and her dressing and closet space.

Imelda needed what I call a total burn down. We should have dug down to the root causes of her problem. We might have created separate spaces for at least one of the activities happening in the room. We definitely needed to sort her clothes, group them by type or season, and thin out the clothes she no longer wore or needed. All of these steps would have made things easier to find and would have stopped the creeping clutter.

I like the phrase "total burn down" because it is a word picture of razing and building back up. It implies that you must start over and deal with each item. If Imelda had been amenable to addressing her issues and to problem solving, we could have built her some lasting systems for preventing clutter. However, because she was only willing to do some housekeeping, she didn't experience the change that is possible with an authentic discovery process. A total burn down is a thorough but nondestructive commitment to deal with your disorder!

Please note that I do not recommend solving your organizing problems by tossing a match into your messy rooms! A total burn down is a dedication to face the music and deal with *all* your stuff. Tim thoroughly dealt with his disorganization, touching every single piece of paper in his office, making decisions, and establishing new structure for going forward. Today, Tim is reaping the benefits of his total burn down.

13

Take an Aerial View

Ever since I was a little girl, I have been flying in small airplanes. My dad has owned several planes in his lifetime, and we fondly call his Cessna 206 floatplane Big Bird. I practically grew up in Big Bird. Flying in and out of small lakes and rivers for fishing and camping adventures, I had the true Alaskan experience. We landed on water, floated down streams, pitched our tents on sand bars, fished for king salmon, and roasted s'mores.

With my float vest on, I've spent countless hours peering out plastic airplane windows, watching glassy lakes and expansive tundra pass beneath me. From the sky, I've slipped past bluish glaciers and green mountains and gushing waterfalls. I've seen caribou collecting by the hundreds, moose meandering in marshes, and beefy bears lumbering along graveled beaches, all appearing like tiny plastic animals on a playing board. While floating down rivers and camping, I've seen all three animals up close and held my breath in the presence of these ominous creatures. Up close, the wildlife and the landscape are raw and even frightening. From above, however, I can catch a glimpse of how all of God's creation is furiously flowing and lazily lumbering at the same time.

Sunsets and sunrises are glorious from the air. I've seen lost plane wrecks, mysterious cabins in the middle of nowhere, and other treasures you can't see from the ground.

In the air, you rise out of your limited point of view, and you can see for miles. A different viewpoint can fill in the gaps of your own narrow perspective and provide a more complete awareness of your surroundings. When we are on land, we have tunnel vision without even realizing it. We can only see that which is right next to the road. We are like ants in an anthill. Seeing the sights from the air affords the opportunity to see the big picture without limits.

Land Use

When Trevor takes me flying around our area, the first thing I notice about our neck of the woods is how much land is used for agricultural purposes. The patchwork of fields stretches for miles and miles. I marvel at how many farmers must still be in operation today to plow all those fields and pick all those berries and harvest all those trees. From Christmas trees to hay to vegetables to grain to grapes, this fertile land grows just about everything in abundance. The countryside is green, populated with trees and bushes, rolling with meadows, divided by rivers, and dotted with lakes. In case you've never been to Oregon, it is idyllic.

When I first began organizing homes and offices, I realized that to truly understand the landscape of organizing problems, we first had to understand how a client was using his or her space. Just as people use land for different purposes from agricultural to industrial to commercial to residential, we use living and working spaces to meet various needs.

When people begin organizing a room, they sometimes make the mistake of walking into it with their blinders on. They ask how to put things away and what containers to use. They look at each room individually without comparing one space's use to the other spaces' uses. They look around instead of looking down.

I tell my clients that we are going to take an "aerial view" of their home or office. I try to help them remove themselves from experiencing their living and working space, and I invite them to make observations about their space from an outsider's perspective. Instead of asking them about what we see, I ask them about the purpose of the space and how they are using it now. What I found was that many people have never defined the purpose of their space. When you pretend you are looking down on the space, you begin to see things you never saw before. By taking an aerial view, you can escape your antlike perspective of your own hill.

Space Tour

After assessing clients' organizing needs, I invite them to take me on a space tour of their home. The space tour is the way we conduct our aerial view of the space. If clients hire me to organize the whole house, a tour makes perfect sense to them, and they gladly act as tour guides. If, however, I've been hired to organize only one space, like a closet or a pantry, the client may be stumped by my request to see the whole house. In fact, some people ask if we can just skip the tour step and dive into the work. To them, a tour of their house seems like a waste of time. In fact, a space tour is an essential launch to a good organizing process.

Gina called me in to organize her master closet. She wanted to surprise her husband by finally dealing with a space that they fought about frequently. It was overflowing with old clothes, and she was ready to purge. She was anxious to begin the project the moment I walked through the door, and she impatiently tapped her foot while I engaged her in an intake assessment. Even though she knew when she booked the appointment that we had a proven process for creating long-term change, she was itching to get to the hands-on work.

She looked rather annoyed when I asked her to take me on a tour of the space, and she exclaimed, "We're just doing the closet!" "I know," I told her. "I promise this won't waste your time—just trust me." She quickly spun me through the house, and I made notes as we went along. In every room, I noticed the belongings of her teenage girls. They seemed to live in every room! We landed in Gina's master closet a short time later and began work.

As we started emptying her closet of clothes, I came across several duffel bags. As I dug through the bags, I found them filled with paperwork. Envelopes and plastic zippered bags contained piles of paper. I found Gina's checkbook and a stack of unpaid bills. We found layers and layers of paid bills as well, all shoved haphazardly in bags in her master closet. I looked at Gina and smiled. I teased, "Look, here's your home office!" Gina laughed and then thought a moment. She said, "You're right! Nowhere in the house do I have a home office. I don't have my own place, so I guess I just store my stuff in here."

I gently shared my observations that her daughters had taken over every room in the home. Instead of carving out space to run the household operations, she just took the only space that was left—her own closet!

As we grouped her clothes and designated giveaway items, we chatted about how much she would enjoy reclaiming her closet for its intended purpose instead of using it as a storage space for her nomadic office. It wasn't even functional because she would haul the bags down the hall into the kitchen to pay the bills, attempt to process paper, and then haul the remnants back to the closet. If Gina wanted to find a needed document, she had to sift through a growing number of bags, and half the time couldn't find it anyway.

The growing demands of Gina's teenage girls had displaced an important household function (bill paying and paperwork). Suddenly the wisdom of the space tour made sense to Gina. When I left, Gina was invigorated by her newly organized closet and empowered to claim household real estate for a home office.

A space tour is best guided by an objective party. Just as Gina was unaware of what her closet bags represented, most people don't naturally self-assess how they use their space. People who live or work in the environment are going to have a hard time asking themselves questions and discovering habits. An outsider's perspective will help them stand back and assess their use of space and observe their pattern of living.

Before beginning a home organizing process, I must know how the whole house flows and how the residents use each room. In the space tour, my goal is to evaluate the entire space and how each room works. I am looking for hidden activities and where stuff is used and stored. I also try to learn how the family would like to be using each space.

Another primary goal of the space tour, however, is to discern some less obvious issues. In the tour, I want to observe the patterns and habits within the home or office. When most people think of organizing a space, they think of creating a place for everything, which is useful of course, but this approach doesn't address the people who use the space. When I organize a living or working environment, I want to truly understand *why* the people use the space the way they do, and I want to discover their needs and work with their natural habits to create a space that makes sense to them. In order to do so, I need to understand how community is functioning and how communication is working in their environment.

Centers of Community

From the air, I am fascinated to observe people's behavior. From the observation window of a Cessna, I think about the people below and why they are grouping together or living apart. Why are some areas more populated than others? Who lives in those less-occupied areas, and what do they do for a living? Are the people in those remote locations farmers or retired or hermits?

In ancient times, people gathered around a water source or under the protection of a mountain or trees. Not much has changed, I've concluded, at least in our area. I peer out the airplane window and notice that the wide rivers create lush valleys where people group to enjoy the fertile land. A community springs up, and then a town, and then a city thronging with activity. A lot of people become bunched into small areas as they huddle together for community.

The same thing happens in a home, really. People are built for relationships, and we gravitate toward one another. For example, adults spend most of their time in the kitchen, preparing meals, eating, and cleaning up, so they are often stuck in that one room for long periods of time. Their children begin migrating to the kitchen, dragging with them their toys or homework.

Often, our clients are frustrated by the clutter that accumulates in the kitchen, including toys and homework. Instead of extricating children from community, our organizers will often set up a play area for small children or a homework area for older children just off the kitchen. Kids want to be where parents are—at least for a while. If you send them off to the basement, they will likely return within a short time. People move toward community, and you can actually observe these age-driven trends and set up your household to accommodate the changing community needs.

After the teenage years arrive, the kids tend to drift away from the community of their family and toward the community of their friends. They begin to express a need for a space of their own. At that time, families need to recognize the opposing unspoken needs of the teenager: to draw away and to draw near. Families can designate a safe space for their children to be independent but also create appealing family spaces that draw their kids back into community.

From bedrooms to playrooms to kitchens to home offices to family rooms, each space will likely go through different uses as time goes by, according to the need for community. Observant parents will set up the home to balance the needs of all family members, each of whom needs his or her own private space and a place to come together.

Kids' bedrooms, for example, should be designed with the age of the children and their need for community in mind. Storing all the children's toys in their bedrooms doesn't make sense when they are small because they will want to play around their parents. Whenever possible, toys should live where the children use them. As time goes by, however, an older child might like a homework area inside his bedroom so he can have quiet time to concentrate. Before you buy furniture and begin arranging a room, consider your own children's need for community and how they are actually using the room now. Don't set up a room for how you want them to use the space; set up the room for how they actually use it!

A note of caution: Even if your children need alone time, balance their privacy with good judgment and supervision. Our organizers have been in homes where unwelcome visitors are coming in the virtual back door. With the proliferation of garbage on the Internet, and with more and more homes boasting computers in every room, allowing your child unsupervised and unlimited access to the Internet is dangerous. You wouldn't let them stand alone in the middle of a seedy section of town, but allowing them unsupervised, uncontrolled Internet access is even worse. Be selective about the community your child belongs to!

Centers of Communication

From the air, I see that wires on poles still connect most of our buildings. Our towns and cities are connected by wires and cables and conduit so that we can get power and communicate with one another. Each new home or shopping center or business plaza is wired into a global communication system. Our homes and offices, like our communities, need systems for communication.

As he takes me on aerial tours, Trevor points out to me the buildings in which he has worked in various cities. Many of those buildings are central offices for an area communications company. Each community has a central office. Underground wires and wires on poles all converge at these buildings and tie into a frame in large concrete rooms. Each little wire is associated with a home and phone number and is joined together with thousands of other wires representing other households in the area. As communities need a place for communication systems to come together, homes and offices need a place where people can gather around shared information.

Business offices usually have one or more hubs of communication and connection. Large offices have a reception desk and a copy room. When our organizers tackle professional office spaces, we endeavor to understand the clients' use of the communication centers so that we can set up systems to maximize their efficiency. CEOs may not frequent the copy room, but they need a protocol for moving files out of their offices and back to the central filing system, usually via their assistants. Without a centralized place for community-use files, supplies, and reference, office mates would store important items in their individual offices. This would cause fragmented and independent operation. A single hub fosters group awareness and unity.

Like an efficient office, a home needs a communication center. One of my favorite things to create for a client is what we call a household hub. Usually the hub is already organically developing in the kitchen, though most people don't recognize it. Most kitchens I've been in share a common trait: They tend to attract non-kitchen items and paper! Most people walk in the door and dump whatever they are carrying onto the first available surface they find, and that surface is often the kitchen counter! From briefcases to day planners to backpacks to stacks of mail, we offload our armloads onto kitchen surfaces! In addition to these offenders, phone messages, take-out menus, team rosters, permission slips, and a myriad of calendars also land in the kitchen and never move on. These loose sheets are affixed to the fridge, taped inside cabinets, stuffed inside junk drawers, and layered in piles.

My job as a professional organizer is to observe habits and perceive possibilities. The frustrated client sees dumped and abandoned items, but I see frequently referenced items and papers that family members are simply storing within view so they aren't lost. I see a need for a household hub!

The household hub is a central area for family communication and reference. Many homes have a little desk off the kitchen that serves as a household hub. If you don't have a desk, you can clear one counter against a wall and set up a hub of your own. Installing a computer and printer at the hub can be very useful for accessing and updating the family calendar, finding directions and recipes, and monitoring your child's computer usage. With a notepad and pen and a bulletin board and tacks (or even with chalk and a chalkboard), you can implement a simple system for taking and displaying phone messages. Of course, the phone should reside in the household hub for easy access. Family members can sort the mail at the household hub and then move it on to the appropriate place. A few reference books like the phone book, dictionary, thesaurus, or even selected cookbooks can live in the hub as well, depending upon your unique uses for your hub. You can designate an "in and out" location for briefcases, planners, and backpacks under (if you have a desk) or near the household hub. The idea is to create one location for the family to communicate with one another and have access to shared resources.

But what do you do with all that nomadic paperwork that piles up in the kitchen and elsewhere in the house? You need to establish a good filing system for capturing and storing permanent paper. If it is actionable paper, you'll need to decide if you are going to process it in the office or in the kitchen, and set up systems for paper flow. The kind of paper that you'll want to store in your household hub, however, is the kind that you look at all the time—reference paper.

Our organizers love to help our clients establish a household reference binder by gathering all the loose and frequently referenced paper and storing it by type for easy reference. Everything from the soccer team roster to babysitter information to the church calendar to pizza coupons can go in a household reference binder. To learn more about our household reference binder, you can visit our website at www.RestoringOrder.com.

Traffic Clogs

Nighttime offers a whole new twist to the flying experience. As dusk settles in, lights begin appearing all over the city, especially on the roads. White headlights and red taillights begin to illuminate the roads as rush hour pulses below. Snakelike processions fill the streets and highways. I can begin to pick out areas that experience heavy traffic and long lines. Traffic accumulates around the most populated areas. Clogs occur when too many cars congregate in one area or when access to those areas is limited and prevents easy flow.

As we all know, our living and working spaces suffer from clogs as well. If our homes and offices were not set up with usability in mind, if we've outgrown our interior infrastructure, or if clutter creates hot spots of disorder, we experience congestion. You can prevent this if you plan your space before you move into it.

We love to have clients call us when they are getting ready to build or remodel a house or office space. They want to consult with us before they frame the space and place furniture. Having experienced unworkable space in the past, they have resolved to get it right this time! When we organize a space from the blueprint or framing stage, we can consider the people using the space, build for expandability if necessary, and prevent clogs from happening.

Unfortunately, most organizing projects don't get to start from the ground up. Usually people call in a professional organizer when they have issues with an existing space and the mess within it. Just as an aerial tour of land will reveal blockage and hot spots, an aerial tour of a home or office will do the same.

Some clogs are simply caused by lack of maintenance, like kids dumping their shoes all over the house or workers leaving messes in a copy room. A regular maintenance schedule can usually resolve these clogs. When a clog begins to have a negative impact on your quality of work or home life, it's time to deal with it and reclaim your space.

Remember Gina, who didn't have a home office? Not having a dedicated office caused her closet to become clogged with bags of paper. Remember the items that we all dump in our kitchens? Blocked kitchen surfaces make preparing and cooking meals difficult. If eating out becomes easier than dealing with the clutter, then the clogged kitchen has altered your quality of family life, and you should address the clog.

Enlist a Tour Guide

We've seen that an aerial view is a tour of your space that can show you the reasons behind your disorder from an objective perspective. When Trevor and I fly together, he is busy charting our course and ensuring our safety. Perhaps the reason why I have so much time in the air to think about the people below is that I'm not flying the plane! When you are living in your home and working in your office, you have blinders on. You are focused on getting through your day and fulfilling your responsibilities. You aren't in a place to be objective, observant, and reflective. That's what the tour guide is for! If you need assistance for your organizing journey, enlist the help of a tour guide—an experienced professional organizer.

A lot of people are overwhelmed by their disorganization. They don't even know where to begin. Asking for help just seems like one more thing to do on their long, long list. Like the wildlife I saw as a child, your disorder can be threatening up close. From a distance, however, and with an objective guide, you can limit your fear and begin to understand the causes of your disorganization.

14

Purpose Your Space

In the last chapter, we discussed the importance of taking an objective perspective of your space and examining how you use that space. In this chapter, we will discuss centers of activity, assigning a specific purpose to each space, and sensible storage. I will share with you how to avoid the black holes of disorder. You will finish this chapter with a secret weapon: the Only Policy. Our professional organizers use the Only Policy to restore order to homes and offices across America, and you can use it too.

Centers of Activity

I've shared how much I enjoy looking out the window of an airplane and musing about the people below. All those people buzzing from their homes to their jobs and back to their homes are fascinating to me. In the previous chapter, we discussed how centers of community and communication develop in personal and professional spaces just as they do in land use. In this chapter, we will address centers of activity in home and work environments to complete our understanding of space usage.

Most of us are familiar with the typical division of land into industrial, commercial, or residential zoning. If we limited our understanding to the three common zones, however, we would miss out on the richness of life on land. With ships sailing in and out of ports, airplanes touching down and taking off, and trains pulling in and out of stations, we must dedicate certain land to the transportation infrastructure. Open spaces like river banks, beaches, parks, and meadows are devoted to outdoor recreation and camping. Sports arenas and fields host competitive physical activities. Amusement parks, roller rinks, and video arcades are all built for entertainment. Churches and places of worship also don't fall into any of the traditional zones but serve to enrich our spiritual lives. Just as we use land for different activities, we can use spaces in our homes and offices for specific activites.

Consolidate Activities

Many people don't realize that widely spread activities may be causing their disorganization. As we evaluate the activities that take place within a home, we will likely find that some activities occur in multiple locations. If, for example, your children play with toys in the kitchen, playroom, family room, bonus room, and their bedrooms, you are likely to have toys strewed throughout your home. You will not find a long-term solution to this problem until you designate only one or two locations where the children will play with and store their toys.

One way to keep toys from traveling throughout your house is to decide that toys that all the children share will live in a community area, but special toys for each child will live in bedrooms in safe spots. If all the children play with board games, action figures, trucks, and dress-up clothes, those toys could be located in a community-use area such as the playroom or bonus room. However, special stuffed animals or models that have been carefully assembled could stay in each child's bedroom for their protection and individual use.

Consolidating activities into specific areas also clarifies the use of surrounding rooms. Once you have corralled the toys into the playroom and the bedrooms, you can reclaim your kitchen, family room, and bonus room for their intended purposes. The point is to be purposeful about what activities you will allow in which rooms so that your household doesn't get hijacked by clutter.

Reclaim Adult Space

Believe it or not, sometimes the parents are the ones who don't want to limit the locations where the children play with and store their toys. Even though the parents are frustrated by their disorderly home, they won't take action. Intentionally or unintentionally, they are giving their children free reign of the household. As a result, toys, games, puzzle pieces, stuffed animals, and Play-Doh roam throughout the house. I've been in homes where the children played with their toys in the parent's master closet! Parents who want to reclaim their household and their sanity can designate some space as "adult space" so that the children understand which rooms are dedicated to them and which rooms are off-limits.

I've observed that children thrive when they know their boundaries. They are more likely to take responsibility for their belongings (when they are old enough) if they have special space dedicated to them. If they are allowed to take over the whole house, they tend to feel less responsible for cleaning up after themselves. This is partially because if they are in Mom's room playing with their toys, they might naturally think that cleaning up Mom's room is Mom's job (even though they made the mess).

More importantly, I've found that if children do not have limited locations where they use and store their belongings, they don't know where to put things away. When parents tell these children to put their toys away, the children really don't know where to begin. They might pick up a board game with the intention of putting it away, but if they don't know its proper destination, they will simply move the game to a different location or set it down in frustration.

Assign Purpose

Understanding how to "purpose your space" is easiest if we demonstrate with a room that attracts all kinds of objects. The laundry room often has extra storage and can draw in random items from around the house. Of course, most of us store laundry supplies and cleaning supplies in this space. In addition, laundry rooms can attract candles, electronics, outdoor gear, arts and crafts, paint, pet supplies, tools, gift wrap, completed artwork, overflow food, infrequently used appliances, hardware, and on and on.

Many of us have tried to organize multipurpose rooms like our laundry room, but usually we only tidy them. We toss out the trash, clean the surfaces, and square up the piles. We capture the dust bunnies on the floor and may even donate some old things to charity. When we leave the room, we feel more organized. Weeks later, however, the room returns to its original messy state. Many of us are frustrated when this happens, and we tell ourselves that organizing just isn't worth the time and effort because it always seems to be short-lived. Our mistake is that we don't assign purpose to our space to make organizing easier.

Evaluate Space Considerations

To organize a space effectively, you must resist instantly diving in and tidying it. Before you touch anything, you must examine the limitations of the space and evaluate the practical purposes the room will serve. You can start by asking some targeted questions. Is the space so small it will only accommodate laundry and associated supplies? Does it have enough storage to include cleaning and utility items as well as laundry? Is the room located near an entrance, thereby also serving as a mudroom? As you can see from these questions, you build on what you know about the room.

Sometimes size determines use. If you have a tiny laundry room, you can only store laundry and perhaps cleaning supplies in the space. You can't store much else in a 6' x 6' space. The primary concerns would be accommodating ingress and egress, and opening and closing the washer and dryer doors. Everything else, like storing supplies and laundry baskets, comes next. On the other hand, if you have a spacious room to work with, boasting plenty of storage and counter space, you can expand the purposes of your room beyond laundry and cleaning supplies to include an arts and crafts center or a gift wrap area.

You can also add or remove purposes according to the room's location and traffic. For example, if your laundry room also serves as a mudroom, your storage needs would grow as the contents change. Since your laundry/mudroom is located near an outside door, you may want to consider a bench for removing and storing shoes, hooks for storing coats, and bins for stowing gloves.

Assess Quantity

As we discussed in chapter 7: "The Process Principle," good organizing is an organic process. I want to share with you my approach to purposing a space. After I understand the space limitations and storage capacity, the next thing I need to do is assess the quantity of each type of the belongings I want to store. Evaluating quantity before storing anything is essential.

As I tackle a new space, I like to remove all the contents (except furniture and heavy items) and group the contents by like type. Then I can see how much we have of each kind of item and make decisions about storage. Sometimes I won't know what to do about room purpose or storage solutions until I've assessed quantity.

Let's say we're organizing your laundry room. When we empty the laundry room of its contents, we may discover a hefty supply of candles stored in the cabinets. I would ask you if you have stored candles elsewhere in your home. Perhaps you also have a stash of candles in your dining room and in the hall closet upstairs. If so, we would need to make a decision about where they will all live. Should they be reunited and live in one space? Or, do we have a good reason why candles should live in more than one location? (Perhaps you live in a remote location where the power goes out occasionally, for example, and you like to have candles handy in several locations.) If you don't have a compelling reason for storing candles in more than one location, I would recommend to you that we consolidate them into one location to provide easy storage and retrieval. Then we can see the quantity of candles we have and assess what kind of storage we need.

It is in this organic discovery process that we assess quantity. If we were to simply "organize" the laundry room by getting a plastic bin and putting all the candles we found in the bin, we might feel better for a split second, but we wouldn't be doing much long-term good. You would still have candles in three locations throughout the house, and you would be unsure where to put new ones. Your indecision would cause you to continue stashing candles in multiple locations.

When helping you assess quantity, I am not just evaluating whether your group of items can fit into the available storage and whether you want to keep all their items. I am also asking other questions about the items. For example, will storing the candles in the laundry room make less room for essentials, such as laundry and cleaning supplies? With more questions, I try to ensure that this location makes the most sense for storing the quantity of items.

I also want to know if the inventory you have will increase. Will you collect more candles and soon outgrow the space we've allotted? I want to know if you can limit yourself to the stock you have on hand. Will you faithfully use up what you have and only replace them as you use them? By asking these kinds of investigative questions as I go, I am ensuring that you are making the best choice for your household and your habits. Together, we are increasing the likelihood that this new order will last.

If you have taken the time to make these kinds of storage decisions throughout your home, you will reap the rewards on a daily basis. Before you took the time to organize your candles, you probably weren't sure of your inventory, and you would have to check all three locations to find a specific candle. You might not know when you are getting low on your supplies and need to purchase more. One common cause of disorganization is not assessing quantity and having a selected location for each type of belonging.

Define a Theme

"Purposing" is simply the process of being intentional about how you will use each space in your home or office. It also helps to define a theme of each space. I'm not talking about turning your home or office into a theme park. I am suggesting that a simple theme for each space may help family members or coworkers remember how to use the space and what kinds of items belong there.

Recently I worked with a family that wasn't spending time together. They were rushing to and from work and school, scarfing down their meals standing up in the kitchen, and not spending much free time at home. The sad thing was that they all wanted to enjoy one another's company and spend more time relaxing. As I walked through their space on our aerial tour and learned more about them, I found that they all would like to play cards and board games together. Not surprisingly, their cards and games were spread throughout the house. Their games weren't easy to find and use, so they simply didn't spend time enjoying them.

As I toured the great room just off the kitchen, I noticed a lot of built-in storage around the television that was mostly unused. When I asked about the space, I learned that the family never really moved into the cabinets because they had intended to use the space for VHS tapes, DVDs, and CDs. As the digital age changed their habits and music and movies became downloadable, they didn't have as many tapes and disks to store. They were no longer using the cabinets for their intended purpose, so the space was relatively wasted. Due to their busy lives, they never slowed down to reclaim the space for a useful purpose. This was a shame because the family just passed through the great room instead of enjoying the space.

I suggested that we give the great room a theme of "family entertainment" to purpose the space. The family thought this was a good idea, and the possibilities began to excite them. We found all the board games and cards stowed in dark closets throughout the house, and we dug up a cribbage board and chessboard from the basement. We used the cabinets in the great room to store these games so they could reestablish family fun in a practical location. In so doing, we reclaimed the great room as a gathering space. With their cards and games nearby, they were more inclined to dedicate time to family entertainment.

These days, if you stop by this family's home on Friday nights, you will smell popcorn popping and hear outbursts of laughter as the family reconnects with one another. They have even begun to draw others into their family activities as the kids invite their friends for an evening of fun. Defining a theme for your rooms can help you repossess storage space, reclaim underutilized space, and create centers of activity.

You can define the theme of almost any space in your home or office. Some spaces, like the family room we just discussed, carry obvious possibilities for themes. Storage spaces, like closets, are not as clear. If you've decided to store gift wrap and streamers and extra gifts to give in your upstairs hall closet, you may want to theme your closet as the party closet. As you organize your home, you may find stray items that you now realize belong in the party closet.

Just like homes, offices can benefit from purposed, themed spaces. In most large office spaces, a room or closet or basement is a dumping ground of abandoned items. Used and dusty file folders, plastic trays labeled a thousand times over, and random desk components usually populate this haphazard space. Some of these supplies could be recycled and repurposed. A lot of purging can take place in a space like this! Once purged, however, it needs a theme so that it doesn't attract archival client files and other unrelated items. I like to theme this wonderland of antiquity the "lost office supplies" room. With an appropriate theme, the room is purposed for containing reuseable office supplies and equipment, and you avoid dumping. With a funky theme, office inhabitants are more likely to know about the lost office supply room and make use of this treasure trove!

Create a Floor Plan

As you are purposing your space by defining themes for each area, you will want to write down your decisions. I find that drawing a simple floor plan is helpful (one page per floor) with each room labeled with its purpose or theme. It doesn't have to be a work of art; the idea is to capture the purpose(s) of each space. The great room might be on the main floor and be labeled "Great Room: Family Entertainment." The laundry room might be located in the basement and it might be labeled "Laundry Room: Clean and Craft." Of course, if you can't think of a theme, you can just label the room and its intended purpose, like "Hall Closet: medicine, paper goods, and linens." Naming the room and the purpose or theme on a floor plan will clarify where certain items should be located.

You can apply the same methods to an individual room as you do to an entire home. When I am finished organizing a garage, I draw out the space and storage cabinets from an aerial perspective. I like to name the walls A, B, and C. (D is the garage door!) Then I note the contents of each cabinet. The left wall (A) might offer a workbench, hand tools, and cleaning tools. The back wall (B) might contain automotive, electrical, and utility cabinets. The right wall (C) might store recycling bins and cabinets for gardening supplies. This floor plan reminds the homeowner of the decisions we made and purposes we assigned.

Wait to make this type of room floor plan until you have evaluated the space considerations of each room and have sorted your items by type. Make sure you've assessed the quantity of your belongings that you intend to store in each room before you make a floor plan. If you impose a floor plan onto a space before you know the possibilities with the space and the quantity of items you intend to store, your plan is unlikely to prove practical.

Avoid Black Holes

When your space has formerly served as a catchall, determining its purpose becomes more difficult. Defining the purposes of these areas is an important step to unraveling disorganization. These mystery rooms contain too much stuff, stymie the organizing process, and make maintenance impossible. Purposing only one room won't do much long-term good because if the rest of the home is disorganized, the messy surroundings will behave like black holes.

Apparently, the scientific debate about the true definition of a black hole is ongoing, but from what I gather, a black hole is basically the remnants of a huge star that exploded. The star's matter collapses into a void. Its gravitational field is so strong that it acts like a vacuum, sucking in matter and preventing even light from escaping. You may have a room in your home or an office that acts like a black hole. If you have one room that is pristinely organized but no further organization within the home, eventually the gravitational pull of your chaotic surroundings will begin to chip away at your island of order.

In office environments, cubicles or offices that have become black holes of disorder are easy to identify. A swirling sea of confusion lies within. Mounds of paper, and junk are layered thick. The resident employee is not always visible among the piles. Coworkers hesitate to hand off projects to the black-hole inhabitant, fearing that they will never see the project again. Black-hole employees are often reprimanded, prevented from advancing, or eventually fired. No one gets much done inside a black hole.

To avoid black holes in your home or office, you can purpose all your rooms. Any area that is left disorderly can begin to act as a vacuum, sucking in other "unknown" items. Armed with your floor plan and room descriptions and contents, you can begin to reclaim your space and your life!

The Only Policy

I would like to introduce to you the secret weapon of Restoring Order professional organizers: the Only Policy. Remember the problem of the traveling toys spread throughout the house? When you limit the locations where kids can use and store their toys, you bring clarity to your home. But how do you enforce this newfound household order? With the Only Policy!

You spent time to think through which toys should live in the children's bedrooms. You have good reasons for simplifying the location and storage of toys. You are a savvy parent who enlisted their help in separating shared toys from individual toys. Together, you placed their individual treasures in their bedrooms, and you explained that these toys were off-limits to their siblings. Your children beamed with pride as their rooms were de-cluttered and repopulated with their own special books and toys. That was last week. Now, trucks and dolls and dress-up clothes have stealthily infiltrated their rooms once again. Before you throw your hands up, try the Only Policy.

This example presumes that your children are a certain age, but you'll get the gist. Tell your children that *only* their special toys get to live in their bedrooms. Emphasize the word "only." Explain that their special belongings will stay safer in their bedrooms. Only their toys and books that are uniquely theirs get to live in their bedroom because they are special. As you engage them in the process of extricating the community-use toys from their bedrooms, explain that *only* shared toys live in the playroom. As you pass the living room on the way to the playroom, reinforce the idea that shared toys don't live in any other room but the playroom. Playfully ask: "Do the shared toys belong in the living room?" Help them with the answer: "No! They only live in the playroom!" As you pass the kitchen, ask them: "Do the shared toys belong in the kitchen?" By then, they should gleefully answer, "No, they only live in the playroom!" End by distinguishing their special toys from their shared toys. Repeat this until their behavior changes.

This training process is easy to understand when we apply it to children, but it works for adults too. If you have trouble with processing paper and paying bills on time, a retraining process is in order. After you've set up an appropriate bill-paying center, you still have to train yourself to use it properly. As you are about to lay down a bill on your desk and shuffle it aside, ask yourself, *Does this live here?* Answer yourself, preferably while no one is listening, *No! It only lives in the to-pay tray!* Then, set that bill in the to-pay tray until bill-paying day comes and you sit down and pay your bills. Of course, you must support your training process with good systems and a schedule of maintenance to succeed.

I know this mental game can sound silly, but I'm here to tell you that it works. The Only Policy is a behavior modification tool that works because it solidifies in your mind the decisions that you've made. It also prevents stashing because it limits the contents of each space to a few types. If you know that *only* laundry, cleaning, and art supplies get to live in the laundry room, then you will be less likely to stash unrelated items in that room.

The Only Policy also limits the locations in which you are allowing yourself to store a single item. If you know that candles only have one centralized home in the dining room, then you will be more likely to walk toward the dining room when you get a new candle as a gift. You now know that the dining room hutch is the *only* home for candles.

I invite you to try the Only Policy yourself. Try it on for size and see how it works for you. Remember that the policy works to reinforce systems you've taken the time to establish; it won't create order for you. It strengthens decisions you've made about storage and trains you to maintain newly found order.

15
Getting Started

One task I personally find confusing is categorizing, storing, and labeling digital pictures. Now that we have both hard-copy photos and digital images, creating and maintaining a system for input and output of memories in different media is challenging. I like putting hard copies in albums and enjoying the memories by physically handling them. I've tried several solutions and changed my mind a few times. I'm checking out my online options for photo storage, thinking about my scrapbooks, and getting closer to a solution that makes sense for our family. Even a professional organizer has organizing issues that she doesn't immediately know how to handle.

I may want to continue using the old-fashioned cameras or I may transition entirely to the digital medium. Maybe I'll get there, but maybe I'll keep using both media. My process is organic. I am in the process of discovering what makes sense to me and what is important to me. Since I haven't had experience yet with an online photo storage option, I haven't made the transition yet. Maybe I'll try it and like it; maybe I'll go back to the hard copies.

I may not know how to handle each issue that comes up right away, but I face the issues head-on and work with them until I discover a system that makes sense for me. The key to getting started is the commitment to begin regardless of whether you know all the answers or change your mind later. You cannot succeed if you won't begin. You will stay in the prison of disorder until you decide to break free.

When we begin organizing, we shouldn't expect a letter-perfect planning process. We can get analysis paralysis when we are considering starting something new, especially if we are afraid of the process or the outcome. This paralysis can prevent us from getting started on projects that are meaningful to us and that will offer positive life change.

Assess, Don't Plan

My guess is that you want to get back in the driver's seat of your life. Being disorganized causes a negative impact to your life, and you want to turn things around. Whether you need a touch-up or a total overhaul, it would be natural to presume that you need a plan for addressing your disorganization.

Game Plans Don't Work

Sometimes our organizers are asked for a game plan for organizing a project or an entire house. People often want a detailed how-to plan for solving their problems. We don't give game plans. Why? They don't work! This may come as a shock, but read on.

Regardless of the project we may be facing in life, we receive the same tired, commonly accepted advice: Make a plan, break it into parts, and implement the plan. For many projects and situations, this can be sound advice. In my real-world experience with disorganized people, however, this advice just doesn't work for at least five reasons.

First, for those who are already up to their eyeballs in clutter, the thought of sitting down and making a game plan to tackle their entire home or office would push them over the edge of sanity. The desperately disorganized are stymied as where to begin. If they were to force themselves into making a plan, they would likely get stuck in the details. If they knew where to begin, they would have already begun!

The second reason that game plans don't work is that people in chaos might use the creation of a master game plan as a stalling technique. When I don't want to do something, I accept almost any substitute for work as a welcome diversion. I can find hundreds of little tasks to occupy my time instead of the big hairy project that looms ahead of me.

The third reason that game plans are unlikely to work is that, believe it or not, many disorganized people are disguised perfectionists! They really want their environment or time or paper to be perfect, but they can't make it perfect on their own, so they give up. Making a game plan would seem like an insurmountable task to perfectionists, and they could spend a lot of time ensuring that the document was standardized and color-coded before they began work. Perfectionism can prevent or stall game plans from working.

The fourth reason game plans aren't viable is that organizing is an organic rather than a preplanned process. I could spend a lot of time with you making a plan for organizing your home, but what if your goals change midstream? What if the purpose of one room changes because of the work we've done in another room? As we've discussed on several occasions, organizing is a dynamic process. We discover things about ourselves when we organize, and our eyes open further and further as we progress. We learn about the contributing causes of our disorder and our own habits. We make changes to our environment as we become more skilled at interpreting our own needs and lifestyle habits.

Lastly, most people don't have the time or desire to create a game plan. If they only have a few projects to tackle, a game plan may seem like a waste of their time. If they have a whole house or office full of projects, they may rightly question how an imposed, premature game plan could possibly take their life and work style into account.

My feeling is that we need to tackle organizing problems head-on and create visible, tangible results as soon as possible. Why dedicate time to making a plan when you can dedicate that time to making progress? If you truly want to reclaim your space and your life, you will have to move from intellectual commitment to actionable commitment. Planning has limited value, but execution begins your process! Now, before you think that I am recommending blindly jumping into the organizing process with no information about problems and needs, read the next section on assessments.

Assessments Do Work

The first thing our organizing consultants do when we've arrived at a client's home or office is conduct an intake assessment. We want to help clients tune into the reasons behind their disorganization. As we begin the assessment, some of our time-sensitive clients are a bit antsy. They want to dive into sorting and purging, and they wish that we could sidestep the assessment altogether. I can appreciate their impatience to conquer their clutter. Usually they've tried other haphazard solutions that have failed, and they've waited a long time for true change.

These clients expect us to immediately take aim at their clutter and blow it away. They want to stand with the troops and watch their disorganization fall like an enemy! We simply encourage them that understanding their own issues is more than half the battle—it *is* the battle! When they begin responding to the questions, they settle down and begin making discoveries about themselves, their roles, and their responsibilities. Taking the time to assess how you got where you are is actually an empowering, enlightening exercise.

To begin your own assessment, you will want to evaluate what your disorganization is costing you personally and professionally. Identifying all the various costs of disorder on your life can be very motivating. As you see the financial waste, strained relationships, or daily frustrations, you will become inspired to ditch the debt of disorder and reclaim your peace of mind.

Next, get out your thermometer to take your disorganizational temperature. What are the symptoms of your disorganization? Is the disease of disorder evident in your paperwork? Is your time infected with chaos? Is your messy environment showing feverish signs of your clutter? Once you have identified your symptoms, you can begin to diagnose what has caused those symptoms. Don't prematurely begin applying medicine without knowing your disease.

Next, you can examine the bottles and salves in your organizational medicine cabinet. What have you tried so far to mask or treat your disorganization, and why didn't it work? Have you enlisted an equally disorganized friend to help you dig out, only to be frustrated by having the blind leading the blind? Have you read books and magazines, applying their advice haphazardly to your wounds? Any good doctor would want to know which self-help cures you had tried if you came in to a clinic with a chronic problem. The task before disorganized people is either to accurately diagnose their own causes and attempted treatments of disorganization or to enlist the help of someone who can.

An assessment should address the scope of the project in broad terms as well as diagnostic terms. You need to find out what you will need in order to conquer your disorganization. This is not a detailed game plan but rather a self-evaluation. What kind of support and resources will you need? Do you need an accountability partner? (I highly recommend that.) Will you need to schedule multiple dates with yourself to work on your projects? (Yes!) Should you dedicate resources to products or professional help? (Possibly, depending on the scope of your project.) By assessing what you will need in general terms, you are being kind to yourself. You are showing a willingness to give yourself whatever you need to ensure your own success. Getting started is easier when your commitment to get organized is paired with an equal commitment to give yourself the support you need.

Complete your assessment by asking yourself what you are going to do next. You don't have to know much more than that to get started. I think more people would experience the liberation organization can bring if they would just choose a place to begin after assessing their situation. This is where the rubber meets the road. Many organizing projects are instantly derailed because disorganized people get paralyzed when they try to decide what to do next. The point is to get started somewhere!

Do What You Know

When I was five years old, I cried my eyes out on the first day of school. I had on my new dress, and my mom thought I would be excited to go meet all the kids. She could sense my fear and got down on her knees to find out what was wrong. When she asked me why I was crying, I sobbed that I didn't want to go to school because I didn't know how to read yet. She hugged me close and told me, "Vicki, that's why you are going to school—to learn to read! No one expects you to know how to read yet!" Ever the overachiever, perhaps I wanted to read so that I could keep up with everyone else. Or perhaps I wanted to save embarrassment. I don't remember the incident except for what my mom has told me. All I know is that fear of the unknown made me want to hide.

Even after you've assessed your organizing challenges and taken stock of your needs, you will need to release yourself to go forward. Sometimes people get stuck before they start organizing, feeling as if they should already know how to solve their problems before they start. Like the five-year-old me, they fear the unknown, or looking foolish, or not knowing the answers. We have to claim our grown-up selves and recognize that not knowing how to organize before we get started is okay. After all, we may not have learned how to organize from our parents, nor is it taught in schools. Organizing doesn't come naturally to everyone.

I have developed a tool to help our consultants-in-training deal with large projects. In turn, they teach it to all their clients to help them overcome their fear of the unknown. It's called Do What You Know. When you are facing a major project, you don't have to know how to solve it. Isn't that freeing? You aren't expected to know the answers from the start. All you have to do is to begin with what you do know.

Begin with the Known

When you begin your organizing process, your role is to be a problem solver. You are the forensic investigator. (For this reason, some people hire an expert to help them. Objectively evaluating their own space and belongings can be hard.) Even if you're working alone, though, all you have to do is begin with what you know about the project. Let's say excessive toys are taking over the house. You may not know anything about dealing with toys. Don't fear! Just begin with the known.

As your kids get older, they outgrow some of the toys meant for babies and toddlers. That's one thing you do know. Gather your boxes and bags and begin collecting all the toys your kids have outgrown. Once you have them in one location, you will notice some feelings emerging. Some toys will evoke sentimental memories, and you might think, *I can't part with that!* Set those aside because you don't know yet what to do with the sentimental toys. Other toys will evoke annoyance as you remember loud sounds they made or how they broke on the first use. You will have no problem bagging up those toys for charity or simply tossing them.

As you clear out the toys to be donated, you notice another group of toys emerge. These toys seem to be in good condition and age-appropriate for your sister's kids. You decide that you will box them up to give to her when she visits at Thanksgiving. After you clear out the hand-me-down toys, you are left with a few odd parts and broken pieces. You can scoop these up and toss them.

Now you can direct your attention back to the sentimental toys. Now that you know your sister will be getting the hand-me-down toys, you feel better about plucking some toys out of the sentimental pile and adding them to the hand-me-downs, figuring that at least a family member will enjoy the toy as your child did. Now, you only have a few sentimental toys left. You could decide to save them for your children or grandchildren (although you don't know whether they will want them in 20 years), but you will have to dedicate space to storing them safely all those years. Alternatively, you could take a picture of them and put them in your child's memory book. This seems to be a happy middle ground that sentimental parents accept. Or you can let them go and create new memories with new toys.

Starting with what you know drains the fear out of tackling a sprawling project. When people have a monster project, they tend to get overwhelmed and give up before they start. You won't have all the answers when you begin, and that's okay. Your job is to start with what you know and troubleshoot along the way.

The Shrinking Unknown

An amazing thing happens as you do what you know: What you know begins to grow and what you don't know begins to shrink! As we step into our projects in faith that they will work themselves out, we enter into a deductive process. From the information we gather, our knowledge grows and our decisions become easier. A little insight leads to more insight. More insight gives you confidence to take the next step. When you step out into what you know, the unknown begins to recede.

The shrinking unknown is something you can count on. I can promise you that if you are willing to simply get started with what you do know, you will experience the growing confidence that hundreds of our clients have enjoyed. Step into the unknown and watch it shrink!

List the Problems

Now you know how to Do What You Know with a project like a house full of toys. But what if you are facing a myriad of projects? How can you broadly apply the policy? In the case of a major project, you can make a list of the things that are not working. Include an inventory of issues in your assessment phase. What challenges are you facing? Are they in your time, information, space, paper, or tasks? Do you struggle with the electronic world as well as the physical world? Even though you may have a long list, getting your organizing challenges off your chest and into writing will feel great.

Remember, you don't need a game plan. You don't have to have a strategy for the whole space. Don't waste your time trying to figure everything out prematurely. That will just cause anxiety and bring up more unknowns. Now that you have an inventory of projects, you can choose the least threatening one on your list if you want. You can start with what you know.

Some people like to start small and generate momentum. Others like to start with their worst thorn. You can start wherever you feel comfortable. The important thing is to start! Whichever tactic you choose, creating a list of issues during your assessment process will clarify your options for starting.

Organizing doesn't have to be stressful and overwhelming. I hope that after reading this chapter, you now feel less pressure and trepidation about starting your own organizing process. I encourage you to spend some time answering the questions in the Assessments Do Work section. Remember that using the Do What You Know policy will give you the freedom to tackle any project with confidence. Begin your dynamic, freeing organizing process today!

16

The Secret to Maintenance

Now that you've reached the end of this book, you know that you must apply organizing truths and principles before strategy if you want your efforts to last. You know that prematurely treating your pain with shortcuts will only mask your problems temporarily rather than providing a long-term solution. In this chapter we will learn how to maintain order. Here's the clincher: If you're looking for a magic cure, you won't find it here. But if you're looking for an ancient secret that works every time, read on.

Keeping Up

Don't you hate unloading the dishwasher? Dirty dishes pile up in our sink and on our counters while Trevor and I play the I Can Outwait You game. We're waiting to see who will buckle first and finally unload the dishwasher. I'm usually the one who caves in because crowded counters and an unusable sink just don't annoy Trevor as much as they do me. I cringe when I start a day by adding my cereal bowl to a teetering pile of dishes. Putting off dealing with repetitive chores inevitably produces incomplete tasks, lingering stuff, and backlog. This backlog creeps up on us and begins to take over our space.

Ongoing tasks like loading and unloading dishes aren't the only things that can cause a pileup in our personal spaces. Special occasions produce extra stuff that invades our environment. The night before Easter, I set out my crosses and bunnies and plastic eggs for the following day's brunch. After the big family brunch, I had my hands full washing the dishes, storing the leftovers, and preparing for my week. As a result, I didn't put away my Easter decorations for two weeks! Though I wanted to put the decorations away, my work priorities took precedence. For a little while, I had backlog in my home because of an event that introduced new stuff into my space.

In addition to ongoing tasks and special occasions, hot spots that emerge and require our attention can cause backlog. My video tapes and DVDs can get messy if we watch them and don't return them to their cases. I hate opening the television armoire and seeing a pile of tapes and empty cases. Have you ever recorded a show on television but then didn't take the time to label the tape? Multiply that by a few recordings, and your tapes can quickly stack up. What a pain it is to go back and fast-forward on a tape until you figure out what show you recorded!

Professional backlog is equally as frustrating and perhaps more costly than personal backlog. Special events that require additional effort to prepare also require equal or greater effort to wrap up. After every speaking engagement, I return to the office with presentation evaluations, requests for service, missorted materials, and a follow-up list. I hurriedly tell my assistant about the event and rattle off the key people to contact while she furiously writes notes. Like a tornado, I return and then spin off to my next obligation.

My assistant (a patient woman approaching sainthood) is left with the backlog. She knows that leads are the lifeblood of our business, and so dropping the ball on the leads could cost us business. Fortunately for us, we have invested the time and thought into establishing clear and organized systems for handling everything from speaking engagements to networking events, so she can shift into high gear and queue the flood of paper for action. As we schedule speaking engagements and appearances, we are conscious of the additional effort they will require and the backlog they will create. We try to anticipate those times and ramp up our administrative staff to meet the onslaught. By being proactive, we can usually prevent feeling overwhelmed by these events.

Most of us, however, don't have efficient systems to anticipate, capture, and manage the invasion of incoming stuff and information. As a result, we become buried by backlog at home and at work. Without proper systems established, we have no effective way to consistently perform follow-through tasks. Whether your backlog is caused by ongoing tasks, special events, or emerging hot spots, keeping up can be hard! Even people who have taken the time to establish systems must be watchful to maintain order.

Discipline Maintains Order

In almost every audience I address, someone asks me, "Once I get organized, how do I maintain it?" The person asking the question is usually grimacing as if painfully aware of the answer she doesn't want to hear. I first tell her that she must embrace organizing as an ongoing discovery process, not a quick fix. Then, she must establish customized systems that make sense to her. Finally, she will need the personal discipline to maintain her new systems.

At that point, I can sometimes hear a collective sigh. Once I drop the D-word, I can feel the disappointment in the room. I can tell that audience members had been hoping I'd slip them the yet-undiscovered panacea that would resolve their mess once and for all. We're all hoping to draw the Get Out of Jail Free pass and avoid having to pay the bail for our liberation from disorder. Books and magazines have promised us that we can have it all in a hurry, so we don't like to hear that good systems supported by daily discipline just might be the answer.

Break Bad Habits

Laundry is a routine, thankless household task that entails gathering, sorting, washing, drying, folding, and putting away clothes. It's the gathering stage that really aggravates me because Trevor cannot seem to locate the laundry bag we have in our closet. Sometimes half his wardrobe is in piles on our bedroom floor!

When we were first married, I tried to convince him to disrobe outside the laundry room (one room away from our bedroom) and toss his clothes in the appropriate baskets. That didn't work. After mounds of laundry began accumulating, I threatened him that if he didn't pick up the piles I would throw his clothes in the hall. He became an expert at stepping over the piles in the hall, and I became more worked up. I even threatened to throw them out the window into the backyard, but I couldn't get the screen off the window.

Then I tried my organizing tactic of working with his natural habits. I bought a lovely sea-grass laundry basket that I placed at the end of the bed to capture his discarded clothes. He never used it. My dog Charlie, however, took a liking to the sea grass and chewed on it relentlessly. I eventually threw the mauled basket away.

Finally, I placed an upright canvas bag on a wooden frame inside our closet. I conceded that he didn't have to leave the room or even sort the clothes; he just needed to aim for the bag. Now that we've been married four years, I'd say that he uses it about 50 percent of the time. This, my friends, is victory! I've given up on punishing him for the piles. I still pluck the rest of his clothes off the floor because his land mines bug me more than they bug him. Call it enablement if you will; I call it self-preservation.

The laundry standoff in our household has wisened me. Very little behavior improvement occurs because of outside influence (like spousal nagging), and we can't force good habits onto someone else (darn!). In addition, orderly living entails more than using the right product. In our case, neither nesting baskets, nor lovely sea-grass baskets, nor canvas bags were the answer. So if the influence of others and the best products on the market won't cause us to maintain order, what will? Not only in my own home but also in my work as a professional organizer, I have realized that becoming aware of and breaking bad habits is one important key.

Choose to Maintain

Living an organized life includes daily choices that create and maintain order. Trevor ultimately has to make a choice to put his dirty laundry in the bag. Then he must make consistent choices to sustain that decision until it becomes a habit. I have explained to him very rationally why throwing his clothes on the floor makes me feel like we are living like wolves, but this has not impacted him. I have explained that this is a hazard, that our small dog could be lost in the mess, and that people who visit may think I'm a hypocrite if they saw how we live in our bedroom. (I'm exaggerating; the situation is not really that bad, but this is one of the arguments I've used). I have begged and argued and probably even cried over his refusal to pick up after himself. From the rational to the irrational, I've tried it all.

In moments of clarity (or perhaps annoyance), Trevor has committed to do better, to pick up his things, and to be more sensitive to my desire to reclaim the floor. At the moment, he means everything he is saying. He intends to do better. But then, at the end of a long day, he is tired and just feels like peeling off his clothes and letting them fall to the floor. In the morning, he is anxious to get out the door and steps over the piles. You can see as well as I can that good choices maintain order, not good intentions! Stay tuned to future books, and I'll keep you posted on the Norris laundry wars! (And if anyone has another tactic that has worked, please e-mail me.)

Remember my annoyance with the video tapes and DVDs that were separated from their cases? Recently I spent an hour watching four "blank" tapes Trevor had recorded but hadn't labeled. I put a Post-it note on each one saying "OK to record over." I reunited the paper cases with the tapes and restored order to our media armoire. This took at least an hour of my time. If we had simply taken the time to write the name of the show and the date on the label when we taped it, I could have saved that hour for something more enjoyable. I am now more committed to immediate labeling of recorded tapes. Next time we tape something, I am going to make a label for it right away! I don't want to have to go back and waste my time watching old shows again!

If we want to begin living in order, we must start by breaking bad habits. Then we must make a choice to change. This decision and the daily choices that follow are really just acts of self-discipline. By choosing to establish and maintain order each day, we are choosing not to be lazy or self-indulgent. We are resisting our natural impulse to set a task aside for future completion or for someone else to complete. Maintenance is simply the discipline of controlling ourselves and the choices that affect our order.

Spending three minutes to unload and reload the dishwasher isn't all that hard compared to cleaning up food stuck to plates and a counter full of dishes. We must retrain ourselves. We jealously guard our time and avoid the chore of dishes as we dash out the door. However, investing a small amount of time now will actually save a larger amount of time later. We are deceived into thinking that we are sacrificing those three minutes, when in actuality we are investing those three minutes in order to save time later! Our choices reflect our belief about the value of maintenance.

The Good News About Discipline

Discipline Is Not What You've Heard It Is

As I've searched for a definition of discipline, I have realized that most of society perceives discipline quite negatively. The dictionary and thesaurus yield ominous, unfriendly connotations. We call it regulation, restraint, obedience, control, authority, and even punishment! One obvious and practical reason why we resist discipline is that we bad-mouth it. When someone is disciplined, we call them regimented or militaristic, implying that those are bad qualities.

When people ask me what I do for a living and I tell them I'm a professional organizer, I get some interesting responses. I can tell some people assume I'm a rigid and uptight person. This used to shock and offend me, but now I just remember that lots of people have a very negative view of organizing.

I wouldn't be a fan of maintenance either if I accepted the popular definitions for discipline. Fortunately, my real-world experience with order and maintenance bears the truth. Creating and sustaining order are actually acts of wisdom and self-protection! Order enables us to live our priorities. It releases us to be prepared, productive, and purposeful.

Order delivers freedom to our lives, and we should want to protect that freedom! As patriots know, freedom isn't free! Just as devoted parents or spouses choose to guard and uphold their commitment in their relationships, we are upholding our commitment to ourselves when we maintain the orderly freedom we've created. Discipline is not the authoritarian you've heard about; it is a means to liberation!

Discipline Transforms

My client's youngest son joined the army when he was 18 years old. He had been a sweet and helpful child in his youth, but he had taken a turn for the worse in high school. He was hanging out with the wrong kids, sleeping half the day, using foul language, and maybe even using drugs. My client had high hopes when her son enlisted. She felt learning proper behavior and respect might do him some good.

At boot camp, the drill sergeant pointed out the boy's bad attitude daily. His superiors did not find his vocabulary charming. He replaced his disrespectful words with "Yes, sir!" Mouthing off earned him push-ups and grueling runs. Sergeants yanked him out of bed early in the morning and worked him hard all day, thus resetting his circadian clock. Even though he initially hated rising early, he began to feel physically better with a regular schedule and exercise. He learned about duty, honor, and personal responsibility that year. His sergeant expected discipline in the little things so that he would be prepared to discipline himself in important things. His selfishness receded as he internalized principles of teamwork and brotherhood. The painful process of boot camp transformed a surly, self-absorbed boy into a stand-up soldier.

When he returned home that Christmas, his family hardly recognized him. He wore his uniform the entire time he was home, proud of his newfound career. He spoke with respect to his parents and called his mother "Ma'am," which tickled her funny bone. If he used food or supplies in their home, he quickly returned them to their place after he was done. While he was home on holiday, he detailed his car, made his bed every day, and helped around the house. Certainly, every child who goes into the military does not always have this kind of an experience, but my client was ecstatic! Her son had finally learned some self-discipline! To this day, her son is a changed man. Introducing discipline into his life changed his attitude and his behavior.

Why does discipline transform us? From the time we are children, we long for structure and boundaries. Any good parenting book (or keen observation) will tell you that totally unstructured, undisciplined children often feel afraid and out-of-control. Popular television shows like *Nanny 911* and *Super Nanny* feature story after story of disobedient, unmanageable children who are transformed by discipline. Structure can calm an unruly child. Children flourish when they know what is expected of them and are given guidelines.

Guess what happens to adults when we live with order and structure? The same thing! From my experience in the field, I can testify that order can transform young and old alike. When I bring order to a chaotic, confusing space or a burdened schedule, I can physically sense the restoration. We feel serene when we understand and control our environment.

The Design for Discipline

Throughout my career, I've experienced the effect of the compelling truths of organizing. I've seen peace arrive once order has been restored. I've shared the thrill of empowerment my clients feel when they press through the Pain Tunnel and conquer their fears. I've deeply enjoyed watching them discover and begin living their life priorities. Organizing their life wonderfully clarifies that which is truly important to them. They begin reclaiming their relationships and setting things right with themselves and with others. They become better managers of their life and their relationships. They start living their potential and claiming possibilities in their lives.

I've always believed that something spiritual is behind organization. A palpable relationship exists between our order and our peace of mind. The painful process grows our character and pays off in the end. The Bible acknowledges that pain is associated with discipline but explains its positive and rewarding purposes: "No discipline seems pleasant at the time, but painful. Later on, however, it produces a harvest of righteousness and peace for those who have been trained by it" (Hebrews 12:11). If we embrace organization as a spiritual discipline, we will receive a reward: The discomfort we experience will yield virtue and peace. Pain is part of a training process of discipline, and peace is the outcome.

We all have the opportunity to exchange our spiritual chaos for peace. God offers the same opportunity in the physical world, perhaps to illuminate this spiritual truth. Those who surrender receive peace. Discipline is an act of surrender. When you discipline yourself to set aside time to tackle your backlog, you are surrendering to the process and resolving to succeed. When you discipline yourself to prune the excess stuff and activities in your life, you are surrendering less important stuff so that you can make room for your priorities. Those who surrender to authentic organization are truly transformed by the process and exchange their chaos for peace.

God designed discipline as a process that trains us, increases our good qualities, and brings us peace. Even though discipline has a bad rap in our culture, its spiritual purpose is to transform us. Maintenance of any kind is difficult because it requires discipline, but its huge payoff exceeds the investment it requires. As I have seen these truths in action, I have become inspired in my own life to practice the discipline I need to have peace of mind. If you are like me and you want transformation and peace, I invite you to embrace God's design for discipline.

The Habit of Discipline Brings Freedom

Perhaps we define organization in overly simplistic terms because we naturally resist the discipline that goes with authentic organization. No one really wants to unload the dishwasher or return clean towels to the linen closet. Training children to put away toys is not very exciting. Some of us procrastinate on these activities and wait until the condition gets critical before we respond. By then we are forced to dig out of backlog, and we find ourselves behaving in a reactive mode. Discipline helps us to tackle unpleasant tasks now so that we can attain something that is important to us: our own freedom.

Practicing discipline in your daily activities yields a lifestyle of proactive, orderly living. Disciplined choices allow you to take control of your out-of-control life. Choosing to proactively organize and maintain your space and time will bring you brand-new freedom. When you streamline your chores, store your belongings sensibly, and clear the floor of obstacles, your environment begins to make sense. As you simplify your space, you can focus on that which really matters to you. When you empty your environment of clutter and distraction, you are free to move on with your priorities.

In the same way, when you limit your activities and commitments to those that add meaning to your life, you will simplify your schedule. As you prune the superfluous obligations that clog up your calendar, you will regain time to think, plan, and act on your own behalf. Organizing your time will create a reserve of hours and mental space to devote to living and enjoying your priorities. As you simplify your calendar, you will recognize and seize opportunities that come your way. Your process for continually comparing new opportunities to your priorities will keep your schedule in congruence with your values.

Retrain Yourself

So the cat is out of the bag. The secret of maintenance is practicing discipline. How can you get from where you are now, buried in backlog and overscheduled, to where you want to be? You will need to replace your false beliefs about organization with the truths you've learned. You will need to retrain your thinking and your behavior. With discipline, you can be proactive and take initiative to manage your life and belongings. When you can think clearly and function with purpose, you can begin to invest in yourself, others, and your dreams. If you want to reclaim your life, reimagine organization as an investment in your freedom.

Self-Correct

We can respond to discipline from outside influences, or we can discipline ourselves by internal influence. Only when we have internalized the value of something do we count it worthy of our attention and self-discipline. Before we are willing to be committed and disciplined to anything, we must understand, accept, and internalize the value of that activity. We are not likely to exercise, grow spiritually, save money, organize, eat right, or do any of the worthwhile activities that require discipline until we believe we will receive a positive outcome if we do so.

We should not be surprised that discipline is necessary if we are to maintain anything that is worthwhile in life, from our health to our financial freedom to our order. Have you ever heard the saying that the best things in life are worth working for? Being a responsible, consistent parent isn't easy. You may often want to scream or give in or give up. Loving and caring for your spouse, an imperfect human, also does not come naturally. In fact, to behave in these ways, we regularly must submit our own natural, selfish desires to the higher good of creating quality relationships. Maintaining order is like that. It is not effortless; it requires repetitive action. When we exercise the discipline of maintenance, we surrender our selfishness or impatience to empower an orderly life. Most of us can agree that the investments we make in worthwhile pursuits pay off in the end.

Once we realize that organizing is worthwhile and will have a positive impact on our lives, we need to do something about it. We need maturity to recognize and deal with issues in our lives that are out of sync with our identity and values. The discipline of organizing acknowledges and corrects the things that are not working in our environment and time. This requires self-observation and action. To correct our organizing problems, we must dig out of our backlog, dig in to set up systems, and commit to maintaining them. Maintenance is an act of self-correction to protect our investment in organizing. Maintenance is our insurance policy!

Expect Tune-Ups

A few years into my business, a handful of my old clients started calling me and confessing that they had regressed. They feared they had irreparably damaged their order, and they wanted us to rescue them. At first, I thought this meant I had failed. I concluded that I had not listened well enough to their issues or understood their needs as we devised their new systems. As I visited their homes and offices to get them back on track, however, I was relieved to find their core systems still intact. In most cases, they simply had accumulated some backlog.

In every instance, the clients admitted that they hadn't kept up with maintenance. In one case, desktop piles appeared because the client had run out of file folders and hadn't had time to purchase more! She maintained her systems for a while, but when her file folders weren't handy, she slipped back into old habits. We only needed a few hours to deal with the backlog, restore their systems, and tweak anything that wasn't working anymore.

The clients who had regressed taught me that even though everyone knows they need maintenance, not everyone knows how to perform maintenance. We now work with our clients to set a maintenance schedule before we leave. A maintenance schedule is essential to keep your systems running smoothly. If you've organized your office, you will need daily processing time to manage the incoming paper, weekly or monthly time to pay the bills and file, and an annual time for archiving. If you've organized your garage, you will likely need less frequent maintenance because you use its contents less frequently. A quarterly or bi-annual update should be plenty to maintain your garage order. We've added to our consulting services a "tune-up" in which we survey the areas where clients are backsliding, evaluate the reasons, help the clients dig out or adjust the systems if necessary, and put them back on track.

As a part of your retraining process, you may need to adjust your expectations from the organizing process just as I did. As we've discussed, the process is not perfect. During your initial phase of organizing, you will dig out of your backlog and set up systems. Once you are off and running with your newfound order, however, you can expect varying levels of regression from time to time. This does not mean you are a failure, or that you are incompetent, or that your systems don't work. If you engaged in an organic discovery process, you probably created your systems correctly. Part of the pain in any process is learning through experience what doesn't work and having the guts to hang in there, fix it, and forge ahead.

When backsliding occurs, use the opportunity to do some forensic investigation to determine the reasons and to learn even more about yourself and your habits. If you can't figure out why you've lapsed, consult an objective friend or expert. Perhaps your office maintenance lapsed because your time management has again spun out of control. Maybe you've slipped back into overbuying, and your craft room is accumulating new layers of excess. With a little discovery, you can get to the bottom of your regression and correct the problem. Remember that the answer is not always what it appears to be. Paper piles might be indicative of an out-of-control schedule instead of an influx of paper.

My advice is to determine a maintenance schedule for yourself as soon as you set up systems. The schedule should name the space or project, define the maintenance activity, and schedule follow-through dates. Some of the maintenance will be routine, as in daily or weekly upkeep. You also may need scheduled or impromptu tune-ups to turn your full attention to restoring your systems and making adjustments where necessary. I find this is especially important in paper management systems; they are more likely to evolve and need consistent oversight. Once you have your schedule, calendar some dates for yourself.

Before we complete our work with clients, we actually have them make daily or weekly or monthly or yearly appointments with themselves, depending on the project and level of maintenance needed. If order hasn't come naturally to you, expect a retraining process that includes tune-ups!

Reclaim Your Life

Establishing and maintaining order requires discipline. We discipline ourselves because we believe the result is going to be worth the effort, and we believe in the rewards we are promised. We go through the process of pain and pruning so we can be prepared to live our priorities and unlock the possibilities for our life.

I hope that this book has presented a compelling argument for the positive life impact of organization. By committing to create and maintain order, you are committing to yourself. You are investing in your own quality of life.

The apostle Paul reminded the early Christians to "live a life worthy of the calling you have received" (Ephesians 4:1) and to "live up to what we have already attained" (Philippians 3:16). He was encouraging them to be conscious of their blessings and, out of gratitude, to fulfill their potential. When we order our lives, we acknowledge all that we've been given and release the possibilities planned for us.

Organization is not what you've heard. Quick tips and how-to advice won't help you reclaim your life. Only an organic discovery process that leads to self-awareness will help you create sustainable change. Because you've changed your thinking and your behavior, you will be equipped to oversee your systems and keep yourself on track. Authentic organizing is about self-management and making good choices for ourselves. When you engage in true organizing, you are creating a life of initiative, choice, and purpose. When you get organized, you can make room in your life for the things that truly matter: your life priorities. You can begin reclaiming your life today.

Notes

Chapter Four: No Shortcuts to Order

1. Brian White, "Weight-loss Industry Becoming a Hefty Business," *Philadelphia Business Journal,* August 1, 2003, referencing a 1996 Department of Health and Human Services report, which is currently being updated.

2. Peg Tyre, "Clean Freaks," *Newsweek*, June 7, 2004. (www.msnbc.msn.com/id/5087895/site/newsweek/)

3. Richard Kriegbaum, *Leadership Prayers* (Carol Stream, IL: Tyndale House, 1998), p. 113.

Chapter Five: The Freedom Factor

1. Frederick Douglass, *Narrative of the Life of Frederick Douglass, an American Slave, Written by Himself* (Boston, MA: Anti-Slavery Office, 1845), p. 99.

RESTORING ORDER®
Reclaim Your Life!®

Info@RestoringOrder.com
888.625.5774
www.RestoringOrder.com

To book Vicki Norris, visit:
BookVickiNorris.com

To hire a Restoring Order®
Professional Organizer, visit:
HireRestoringOrder.com

To become a Restoring Order®
Professional Organizer,* visit:
RestoringOrderTraining.com

RESTORING ORDER®
Reclaim Your Life!®
Reclaim Your Office™ Collection

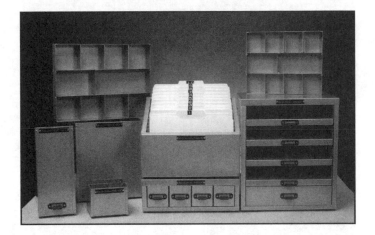

Products@RestoringOrder.com

888.625.5774

www.ReclaimYourOffice.com